MY REALITY OF SPIRITUALITY

MY REALITY OF SPIRITUALITY

SHAYLYN PITTS

Shaylyn Pitts

Contents

1	The Great Awakening	8
2	Spiritual Awakening	10
3	The Beginning	16
4	My Parents	19
5	Kyanon	31
6	Guilt Felt Like Home	35
7	Leaving My Childhood Home	38
8	Pulmonary Embolism	44
9	Rolling Hilux	49
10	I Love You	52
11	Ashamed	56
12	The Crumbling	65
13	Lost and Searching for My Purpose	71
Little Life Update		76

14	The Relationship that Broke Me	77
15	Lion's Gate Portal	83
16	Cracking Me Open	87
17	Lost and Getting to Know Myself	96
Little Life Update		112
18	Phases of Awakening	113
19	My Spiritual Awakening Discovery	115
Little Life Update		124
20	Expanding Awareness	127
Little Life Update		138
21	Spiritual Awakening Challenges	139
Little Life Update		153
22	In Touch with My Higher Self	155
23	A Whole New Identity	160
24	A New Way of Living	169
25	The Good Stuff	178
Little Life Update		186
26	Not the End, the Beginning!	187

This is my reality of spirituality.
Throughout this book, I will explain the series of events and phases that either drew me deeper into my ego or woke me the f*ck up!

Introduction

Firstly, I would like to tell you how this book has come about. Over the past two years, I have been in an intense state of awakening. Many events have pushed me into my spiritual awakening, as I will elaborate on throughout this book. Once I became aware of my own spiritual awakening, I kept receiving synchronicities, repetitive numbers and signs pushing me to write down my awakening journey, with the thought that someday I will guide others. So, over the past ten or so months, I have been noting down things that channel through me – my experiences, realisations, thoughts and feelings – with the slight niggling that someday I might have use for them, placing my trust in the universe, not knowing the reasoning for noting down what seemed like crazy-lady gibberish into my mobile-phone notes.

Today, all these crazy-lady notes have been called into action. I was meditating to a guided meditation, which involves seeing and receiving messages from my higher self. What is your higher self? Your higher self is the fullest you that remains in spirit; it is you in all your awakened glory. The clear-as-day message I received from my higher self was: *Write a book!* I could see it – white, with gold titles. I had the sense come over me that this book is what all the events in my life have been leading me to. I feel like this is my life's purpose, sharing my story to help others.

I pondered on the idea all night. *How will I write a book? Where do I even start?* I decided to pull a card from one of my many oracle decks. 'Angels, where will this book take me?' I asked, as I fiercely shuffled those cards, hoping for a clear answer, and I sure got it! The cards 'Shower of Abundance', 'Follow any guidance you receive', and 'Share your voice' all flew out of the deck at me. *Wow. Thanks.* So here I am, trusting the process, sitting in my bed at 10 pm on a cold May night, in utter shock that me, myself and I are attempting to write a book. With my below-average literacy skills and inability to finish reading an entire book, this is going to be interesting. Wow – 416 words already.

***

Currently, I am a young, twenty-three-year-old female, working part-time for a new-home builder, running my own residential design business, and chasing the spiritual life every spare moment I can. I am newly single. I love sitting on the shower floor – this is where all my greatest ideas and realisations are born. I also love long drives alone so I can sing at the top of my lungs. I think I'm hilarious and often laugh at the things I say (just laughed at that). I love the sun, sand and sea, adventures, and I am all about the good vibes! I am currently living in Melbourne, Australia, with my dad and sister, amongst the worldwide pandemic we call coronavirus. I'm trapped at home and have been in a complete state of transformation, venturing down my spiritual path, finding myself, learning, growing and evolving each day. In this life, I feel like I am so young to be writing a book and telling my story. Aren't people who write books about their lives in their sixties? Well, not now, they're not! This is only the start of my story; the rest is yet to come.

If you had said to me a few years ago that I would write a book, I would have laughed so hard. During school, I hated English, only just passing. I wasn't great at reading and, honestly, I didn't enjoy reading at all. The belief I had within myself that I hate English and don't enjoy it is something I needed to unlearn to get this book flowing. And you know what? Once I unlearned this belief, I couldn't fathom how much I enjoyed sitting down, whipping my laptop out and allowing the words to flow. If I didn't unlearn that limiting belief I had within myself, this book would have never been written.

Everything in this book is my personal experience. I am not pushing my beliefs onto you in regard to the universe and all this esoteric stuff. I am not telling you that this is how it's meant to be. I am purely here to tell my story, to hopefully help you along yours, and give you some peace of mind that, although you may be struggling and life may be testing you, you will pull through stronger! From wounds to wisdom.

***

Spiritual awakening can be heavy, emotional and confusing. I hope you feel my vulnerability and rawness. I hope you find my story relatable, empowering, funny at times, loving and also enlightening. I want you to feel like you can overcome any obstacle life throws at you because you can!

I am always learning, always growing and feeling my way through life. This book is a perfect reflection of my experiences and the way I have perceived them so far along my journey. I cannot wait to look back in ten years or fifty years to see how much more aware I am, and how much my consciousness has shifted; I may even be enlightened by then – who knows! I still have so much to learn – maybe a better way to put it is 'unlearn' – on this beautiful journey we call life.

***

I had so much fear around putting my experiences within

this book, as I didn't want people to be perceived in a certain way. For this reason, you may notice that I have left some names out. My experiences and interactions don't define the people who were involved – they were acting purely through their conditioning. I have nothing but love for these beings and they have been put on my path for a reason. This book is coming from a place of love. It is no one's place to judge.

Before writing this book, being vulnerable was one of my greatest fears. I was so good at hiding my reality, blocking out my emotions and struggling to embrace where I was at on my journey. I wanted to be fully healed already. I wanted to show the world I was healed so I could heal others. You know what I realised? I don't need to be perfectly healed to help others; healing is always going to be a journey. My natural gift is healing, teaching and empowering people on their own journey. My vulnerability will heal you. My experiences will heal you. The awareness you gain from this book will heal you. This is my gift of transformative light I will shine on the planet.

I

The Great Awakening

I want to touch on the fact that currently we are going through the 'great awakening' on Earth. This may sound a bit esoteric; however, I feel it is important – super important – to mention. Countless souls have come to this planet at this specific time to wake up and raise the overall vibration of the planet. If you're waking up, this is you; you are awakening to raise the vibration of the planet. You have a greater purpose, just like me. I know I am here to connect, heal and shed light onto this somewhat dark planet.

I personally believe the current worldwide pandemic of coronavirus that I'm living through is playing a major role in people waking up, as many people are forced to choose between falling deeper into the ego and living in fear or waking up. Just like I was. It has gifted me transformation through some deep struggles. A complete shift in my reality. People have spoken about the great awakening occurring for years, and I've heard many people say that our planet is calling for it. I'm no expert around this great awakening stuff, but I do feel it is important to mention in this book.

I feel that I have incarnated here during this time to assist in this raising of the planet's vibe! This higher vibrational planet means a higher vibe life – higher vibe, living your purpose, manifesting easier and just a more joyful earthly experience. I have come here at this time for a reason. I feel in my soul it's time to birth this book, to help others, and tonight at 21:39, on the 25th of June, I have given into my soul niggling at me and blocked out my ego telling me that, *I'm too busy to write a book*, and picked up my laptop to get some words flowing. Someday, if people do read this book, I hope hearing my story changes your life.

***

The great awakening will invite in a new world.

2

Spiritual Awakening

You may be thinking, *What is a spiritual awakening?* To explain what a spiritual awakening is, I must first define the ego. I believe the ego is a mind-made identity consisting of compulsive thinking. You are unable to control thought and unable to stop it. You identify with yourself through thought – you are the ego, consisting of narratives and thoughts that you identify with, as you, as one's self, who you mistake for who you truly are. You identify yourself and paint a picture of who you believe you are based on the way you look, possessions, skin colour, abilities and knowledge. You derive your sense of self from things that aren't you. You are your thoughts. Ego is the complete identification with thinking. You are your mind. Well, so you think. When I was trapped within the ego mind, I had absolutely no idea I was trapped in the ego mind.

I believe the ego is always seeking the most of something, to be superior to the person next to you, or even your current self. Well, this was the case in my experience. Commonly, the ego will choose to identify itself with its 'best' feature. For example, if you are 'good-looking', you derive your sense of self from your appearance. If knowledge and know-how are your strengths, you automatically define your sense of self as that 'smart person'. When people around you are seemingly more 'good-looking' or 'smarter', your ego feels threatened, resulting in a lower emotion. It's uncomfortable and I found myself questioning my worth in these situations. Nothing serves the ego for long. I was constantly searching for more, reaching for the next best thing, wanting to be more – my ego was never happy.

My ego tended to seek identity and wanted to create this idea of who I thought I was through my career, belongings, the way I looked and my boyfriend. Society fuels this through daily interactions. 'What do you do?' is such a frequently asked question and automatically links our career path to our identity. I noticed some people 'lose themselves' when they retire, and I believe this is because they always identified with their job. They were a 'doctor' – that was their sense of self – and when they no longer can link their identity to their job, they feel lost and lack a sense of purpose.

Society is shaped around the ego mind, and the ego loves to live in a state of fear, lower vibrational thoughts and emotions. My ego mind was drowning in either a fear state, fear of what's next, fear of what people think, or a desire, consuming, wanting more, feeling that I need more to be happy, feeling that happiness will be found in the next 'thing' I desired. This was all ego, not me, not who I truly am. My ego loved to cause pain, guilt and suffering.

When I spoke to myself within my mind – saying things like, *I look bad today*, for example, or whatever rubbish was programmed in my mind – I thought, *Where is this place I am speaking from?* I pondered this thought, and I discovered that there is self/soul/consciousness and there is ego, completely separate from one another; we are pure consciousness, separate from the mind. Read that again, 'we are pure consciousness, separate from the mind'. We. Are. Separate. From. Our. Mind. We are not our minds. Let that sink in.

Underneath your thoughts, you are a conscious, eternal spiritual being. Now that we have established that we are pure consciousness, an eternal spiritual soul, and are actually separate from the mind, I believe this is when awakening begins. Who 'you' are is far beyond what your ego conjures up!

My spiritual awakening occurred when I shifted out of the ego mind and awakened to my soul. I realised that I was not my ego mind and no longer identified with its thoughts, beliefs and narratives. We are eternal spiritual beings having an earthly experience.

Once triggered into my awakening, I started to question everything. This was brought on by extreme emotional hardship, giving me the opportunity to wake up or fall deeper into my ego. I found myself searching for more. I felt lost, confused, and out of place, and had no idea what was happening to me. I experienced heightened anxiety and depressive episodes, making each day a battle, like a war within my internal world, every single day.

Once awake, I moved into a higher level of consciousness and vibration. Now, when I say vibration throughout this book, I am referring to a kind of pervasive life force, where I feel everything we do is a vibrational energic exchange. Some things resonate at the lower end of the scale, such as fear, shame, guilt, whereas on the higher vibrational side, we are looking at willingness, acceptance and love – the top of the vibrational energy is that of enlightenment.

I then discovered that everything in this earthly experience is a direct reflection of me; my thoughts created my reality, and so did my vibration. If I was feeling lower vibrational energy frequently, that is what I was inviting in and attracting.

I became aware that we are all connected infinite souls having a temporary human experience. We are not our looks, possessions or abilities. We are pure consciousness. I feel our number one mission when we come to Earth is to wake up and remember our purpose and why we are here. There are many phases and aspects of my awakening – which often went unnoticed during the early stages – each phase stripping away societal conditioning, drawing me closer to who I really am. Our natural state is that of enlightenment; we must peel away at the layers of conditioning.

I hope this book guides you, supports you and shows you that you are not alone. I hope you can find some clarity and humour in the testing times I experienced. Imagine going through your first ever proper break-up and a spiritual awakening, all amid a worldwide pandemic! Woah! What a party.

This is a life-changing experience. Buckle up!

***

My spiritual awakening was triggered when everything around me that satisfied my ego started crumbling, one thing after another. I was pushed, battered and bruised. I kept pushing back with my ego mind and didn't surrender until I was completely broken down.

Until I became aware of my awakening and decided to change my life, I was purely surviving, definitely not thriving, living in a low vibrational state drowning in fear, guilt and shame. I didn't turn to spirituality from a happy life. Being happy and content within my surroundings never had me searching for more; it was the hard times that forced me to question everything. I experienced increased anxiety, depression, and the feeling of wanting to know more. My old ways of living didn't satisfy me. I felt lonely and like no one understood me. I questioned society, questioned my beliefs. I turned into a hermit. Other people drained me. Relating to people in my life was a struggle. I craved happiness but didn't know where to find it. I was drawn to spiritual practices like meditation and card reading. Searching to find my life's purpose, I was drowning in synchronicities, repetitive numbers and signs. I had an inner knowing that there's more to life and I knew I was so close to finding out what it was.

I feel those who go through turmoil are gifted the opportunity to choose whether they hit snooze on the alarm clock of awakening – staying in that struggle of half-asleep, half-awake, wanting so badly to keep sleeping – or wake the fuck up, realise that they have the choice to shape their lives, open the blinds, feel the sun on their skin and dance to the sound of birds singing. You feel me? If you're woke, then, hell yeah, ya do! If you're bashing snooze on your alarm clock, hiding behind fear, guilt and societal beliefs, then the fact you have read this far is a clear sign it's time to wake the fuck up! Excuse the profanity – I need to get through to you. You have been divinely guided to this book. We don't just arrive on Earth to have a shit one and die! Step out of that painful ego trap and into your soul! Wake the fuck up!

With every traumatic event I faced, I pushed myself deeper into my ego. I could have woken up earlier and saved myself a whole lot of grief if I'd had a book like this lying around or gifted to me. I would have had a greater understanding of things, instead of being completely in the dark, completely unaware, scared and ruled by my ego mind. I am creating the book I wish I'd had during my darkest days.

This is where my spiritual awakening story starts. We will start with the series of events and circumstances that gradually triggered my spiritual awakening, each experience pushing me further into my ego until I finally woke up. Then we will move onto the phases of awakening I have experienced along my journey so far. Then, lastly, I'll explain where I am now, how going through a spiritual awakening has shifted my life for the better.

***

This is my unique journey. This is my reality of spirituality.

3

The Beginning

This book is coming from my soul and it needs to be birthed into this world! The coronavirus pandemic has given me the time to do it! I have opened my laptop again and now I will start to explain my own spiritual awakening, what triggered me, and what got me to where I am today, in the hope that this book finds and helps people who truly need it someday in the future.

As I'm sitting here trying to think of where to start, and what kicked off my journey of awakening, I've realised I don't really feel it was one particular moment for me. I need to just spill my story out onto these pages, all the testing times that triggered my life-changing transformation. I want to take you along for the giant laugh my life has been up until my awakening and even after. I feel it was a build-up, a major build-up. Many testing circumstances and situations occurred to get me to breaking point, and far too many times I chose the path of ego and suffering, keeping my happy face on show to the world.

My mind was my own worst enemy and it had control.

I grew up in Emerald, Victoria, Australia, on a couple of acres, in the hills, with my mum, who was a stay-at-home mum, my dad, who owned a car dealership most of my life, and my younger sister, Ky, who is four and a half years younger than I am. I also have an older half-brother named Luke, who grew up living with his mum. Ky and I were real tomboys, either in the mud or spending time with our cousins playing pranks and getting up to mischief. In my teen years, I was horse-mad. I loved horse riding and had a few horses over the years that fulfilled my young-girl dreams. I went to Emerald High School and I had some great friendships. We always had family Christmas at our place, and I was very blessed to have my extended family around me growing up. Everything seemed all 'happy family' on the outside, and, yes, we did have some great times whilst growing up, but there is more to our family than meets the eye.

I believe my parents played a huge part in what shaped me. I was a fighter, drowning in self-doubt, living the emotionally unstable home life every Cancer Sun (star sign – Cancers are all about a stable home environment) fears. I was always swimming in guilt for some reason, plus many other aspects of my life unconsciously played on loop. I was living in a contracted state of consciousness, with lower vibrational emotions feeling like home. I was constantly let down, abused, emotionally and energetically drained. I moulded this fight mindset and my ability to block out my emotions was my all-time favourite skill up until my awakening. I believed this was a sign of strength. I feel this hindered my awakening from happening sooner; I was stuck in that state of surviving and hitting snooze on the alarm clock of awakening, blocking it out with my ego and pushing myself into a deeper sleep, and deeper suffering. I thought burying my feelings was how to get through things. I had no idea that feeling the pain, letting it overwhelmingly crack me open, would be my greatest gift.

***

My pain was my gift towards growth.

4

My Parents

My journey with my mum and dad is such an important part of my story, and I almost left it out. My fear around making people within this book look not very desirable nearly held me back from speaking my authentic truth, my story and my reality, along with my deeply entrenched fear of becoming vulnerable. I also am afraid that it is so easy for people to view my experiences from a place of hate. But I am coming from a place of love, purely sharing my journey. I am pushing past all this because as we know, great healing lives on the other side of fear. Someone will always be pissed off no matter what we do in life; plus, I couldn't leave out such an impactful piece of my story.

I have been in a state of processing over the past few weeks and I cannot seem to shake the energy that is rising in my body. I feel this may be my inner-child trauma trying to surface from within me, needing to be put onto these pages. I can't avoid it any longer. I need to accept and invite in the fact that I didn't have an amazing childhood like my mother always told me I did. 'Shaylyn, you were very lucky growing up.' She drummed this into me. 'You were spoilt. Look at how lucky you are.' And, yes, in the sense of belongings, hobbies and the home I lived in, I definitely did have it very good, and I have some incredible memories from my younger years. However, emotionally, I have many events and circumstances that I need to heal from. I have now realised that it doesn't matter how blessed you are within your surroundings; if you don't deal with your emotions and the shit going on in your head, you will never be happy. I blocked this out for so long as I felt guilty for admitting the fact that I was miserable for the majority of the time. I shouldn't feel guilty for being honest with myself about how I felt growing up. I shouldn't feel guilty about speaking up about the traumas I am needing to heal from. Admitting this doesn't mean I appreciate my parents any less. I am just purely speaking my truth. I feel writing this is a huge step in the right direction towards my wounds being healed. This is definitely what has been rising in me over the past few weeks. I am feeling the lightness come over me, *Ahhhh, finally, I am on the right track*. All I needed to do was surrender to it, surrender to the universe and trust the niggling feeling telling me to let the words flow.

Something from my childhood that has risen and keeps popping into my mind, as it strongly affects me now, is what happened during my tomboy years. From the ages of about seven to eleven, I was a major tomboy, even more than I am currently. During these years, I was all about playing footy, hanging out with my boy mates and dressing like a boy. It was a phase, and I remember always being questioned by my mum, 'Why do you want to dress like a boy?' And being younger, I didn't really know. I enjoyed hanging around with the boys, playing footy and getting muddy, so, naturally, I wanted to be like the boys. I think my mother questioning me was her trying to make sense in her own mind of the reasoning behind why I wanted to dress like a boy, also probably so she could explain to her friends why her daughter was like this. In my mother's confusion, trying to make sense of this, she started repetitively asking me if I liked girls, and if I was a lesbian. Imagine being a young girl and getting asked that. I didn't even understand it at the time, but it's clear as day in my mind, like it happened yesterday. I felt like I was getting interrogated, and if I was found out to be, in fact, a lesbian, then I would be guilty of something wrong. This made me believe that there was something wrong with this, and I struggled to express my sexuality as I got older, holding myself back and blocking out the way I felt, as I was terrified of others' opinions. After suppressing the fact that I am bisexual for many years, I am now spilling the words out into this book, and learning to accept myself. This is something I never thought I would write about. Even some of my closest mates have never heard me mutter these words, and I'm sure when they read this, it will be a shock, but maybe this is my own unique way of coming out. I find it beautiful that people are going to learn about me in such a real and raw way through reading my story; this is something my voice can't express just yet. My sister and I sometimes would joke with Mum about me being a lesbian. I feel this is our way of slowly warming her up to the idea. Got to give it to her, though – Mum was onto something questioning me about my sexuality. I guess she did always know.

Growing up, I had waves of anxiety come over me when Dad arrived home from work each night. He's a fiery, loud energy, and was full of anger at times. Dad is usually the loudest in the room and this is something that I have always been so sensitive to, especially during my younger years. Before I started writing this chapter, I did not fully understand why I dreaded Dad coming home from work each night, and I felt guilt around the fact that I did not want him to arrive home. It's crazy how, as I write, I realise the reasoning behind things. I love the clarity writing gives me. Dad was often triggered by my mum's excessive drinking, going from 0 to 100 real quick with his rage, yelling the house down most nights with his 100-acre voice. I could never fully relax when he was home and, therefore, I dreaded his arrival. I didn't know when the deep, loud voice was going perk up, sending anxious rushes throughout my body.

My parents would argue frequently, and it left me feeling sick. I just wanted it to stop. I always felt I needed to step up to try to prevent my parents from arguing. I just wanted so badly for them to be quiet, so I often felt like I was crossing the line, being a child trying to ensure Mum and Dad wouldn't hurt each other. This just didn't sit well with me and I hated it. I was like a defuser, always jumping into their arguments and occasional physical altercations right before things got any worse. My parents are fire signs, and I was the water, trying so hard to extinguish two flames. I hated yelling, but somehow it was where I would find myself most nights, angry, upset and yelling, doing anything I could to try to get my parents to stop arguing, or yelling to be left alone. I wanted to escape this. The more I write, the more I heal, and the more I become aware of the lessons I need to learn and resolve with my parental figures.

All I ever wanted to do was impress my dad, but he is a perfectionist, and nothing ever felt good enough for him. Even now, when Ky or I am cleaning the house, or whatever it is we're doing, he will take over midway through, watch us like a hawk, or be standing close by giving detailed instruction on how to complete even the simplest of tasks. He ensures everything is done to his standard, always making our efforts feel not quite good enough. This caused us to feel like we never do anything right, instilling self-doubt within us and crippling our confidence when completing a basic task, and this followed through into our school and work lives, making it hard for us to trust our abilities. I always craved extra direction in school or leaned on those around me because I didn't have faith in myself, because Dad never put that faith in me and my abilities to get a job done. Now I have this same sense of needing to control or take over when I want something done, just like he does.

Through awareness, I will break this habit.

Dad's behaviours and reactions often leave me feeling anxious. Commonly when I ask him to 'please be quiet' because I have an important call or I'm working, he instantly has a fiery reaction, saying, 'You're the loudest in the house,' 'You, be quiet,' 'You, shh,' 'You're never quiet.' I feel attacked for having made a simple request, but this is just the way he is. He can be selfish and inconsiderate at times, and I think this may be why I placed such pressure on myself to make others happy, because I know what it feels like to be on the receiving end of someone who can be quite inconsiderate at times – it does not feel good. I have struggled with our relationship, and had trouble reaching out, opening up and speaking to Dad about more serious topics or asking for help with something because I was scared of his reactive ways. He was so easy to set off, it ended up being easier battling through some things alone.

My mother being an alcoholic in denial has affected me far more than I previously cared to admit. Growing up, it was hard for me. Growing up under the same roof as an alcoholic was too emotionally unstable for me to handle. She was in denial and she had let the ego take over, drowning in guilt, shame, fear, and the good old drink. I never knew what I was going to get each night after coming home from school. Would I get the happy mother or the mother who would sit on the end of my bed tormenting me by constantly asking, 'What's wrong?', as I cried and screamed, 'Get out,' 'Piss off,' and some other choice words? My highly sensitive self needed alone time and peace to recharge and escape the energy that surrounded my wine-fuelled mother, but apparently some nights that was too much to ask. I always felt like she wanted to make me angry, like she wanted to make me snap, and she sure did achieve that. I felt so uncomfortable in my own self because I would have these anger-fuelled outbursts. This wasn't who I wanted to be, this didn't feel good for me, but I was in the environment where I would always seem to find myself back here. Due to my mother's excessive drinking, I struggle with partners and those around me drinking more frequently on weeknights, as I fear patterns from the past may repeat. This is something I am consciously unlearning and choosing not to bring into my future space.

My parents had a messy break-up, and I was depressed and anxious for the majority of the time, and branded 'the abusive teenager' by my mum, as she struggled to deal with her own shit. It felt like my mother had turned everyone against me. My pop would have stern talking-tos with me, telling me to pull my head in, as would my mum's closest friends. My mum would tell me that I needed help, that I had issues, and she made me out to be a troubled child that abused her. You know what? I probably was a troubled teenager that did need help, but instead of painting me as the enemy, maybe getting me some support would have helped? Writing this makes me cringe. Even writing that word 'abused' makes my blood boil. My mum used it way too often, about circumstances that, in my opinion, did not constitute abuse at all. I sure felt like this horrible person she made me out to be. Was she deflecting? Was she deflecting the fact that she had emotionally and psychically abused me time and time again? She needed someone to blame and I was that someone. When she would tell her friends about me, it was her constantly playing victim. My mother seemed to thrive in the victim state, and her teenage daughter abusing her was another way she could pursue this path. Of course, I wasn't an angel. Of course, I had outbursts. I was constantly getting picked at and questioned. I was struggling. I hated my life. I hated living with my mother and I always had rage bubbling below the surface, ready to explode. I was so angry, and she made me so angry. I feel anger is what got me through. I turned so many lower emotions into anger. If I didn't have anger and the use of strength through anger, I don't know if I would be here today.

I will never forget the day my anger reached its highest peak. One night after school, my sister, her friend and I were all hanging out in the kitchen, just talking and mucking around. I would have been about sixteen at the time, and Ky and her friend were about twelve. Mum walked into the kitchen. She was more than a few wines deep and set on upsetting me. She started with the usual picking at me and questioning, and I started to get lippy. I cannot remember what was said that made my mum snap, but she launched at me, grabbing my hair and pulling it with such force that it caused me to fall to the ground. My sister's friend looked at me in shock. I got up and ran to my room crying. I was so embarrassed and I felt so small, but I quickly turned the sadness and embarrassment into full-blown rage. I was fuming, so fuming, kicking my bed, and throwing my phone. I even punched the wall like every angry teenager does at some point. I must have had some serious muscles back then because I didn't even leave a dent in the plaster. I had never been this angry before. I didn't recognise myself. It was definitely a build-up from many other nights of torment, all erupting into one night of pure rage. Once I had calmed down, I finally ventured out of my room late that night, probably because I was hungry (I'm always hungry). I heard my mum on the phone to Ky's friend's mother, the friend that had seen me get pulled to the ground by my hair. I heard my mum telling her that she was sick of my abuse and that she didn't know what to do with me anymore. I was so fucking angry; I was trying to make sense of how she could so easily manipulate a situation in her favour. Things like this would happen so often I actually started to believe that I was an abusive, overpowering, bad person. With her constant twisting of stories, I found it hard to believe anything good about myself.

Another memory has just risen within me just as I was about to close my laptop. I'm emotionally tired, but I know I need to write it out to heal. Here we go. The memory that just popped into my mind was of one of our heated nights at our Emerald home during the time that I couldn't see my dad or contact him due to an intervention order my mother had placed against him. My mum and I were having our average heated argument because, once again, she wouldn't leave me alone. She would intentionally pick at me, try to make me explode, to give her some sort of reaction. And you know what's funny? As soon as I cracked, she was happy, acting confused as to why I was so angry, and then she would leave me alone. This night, she kept getting closer and closer to me. I kept saying, 'Piss off,' 'Leave me alone,' 'Go away,' until she got so close, she pushed me, forcing my back against a wall, and then she pushed me again, so I pushed her back, trying so hard to create some space between me and her wine breath. Before I knew it, she had me pushed against the wall with her hands clenched around my throat. In that moment, I wasn't scared for my life or anything because she wasn't hurting me – well, not that I could feel anyway as the adrenaline was rushing through my body – I was just in pure shock that my own mother was choking me. I couldn't believe it. How had things got this bad? This is a moment I will never forget, as her hands clenched around my throat tighter, pushing my head harder against the wall. We made eye contact and she laughed at me, with this pure-evil laugh. I was horrified. I pushed her off me and ran to my room, swiftly slamming the door behind me and moving my drawers in front of my door so she couldn't get in. The next hour, I cried on my bed while she paraded outside my bedroom door, shouting and screaming, telling me that she was going to call the police on me for my abusive behaviour. *My* abusive behaviour, she reckons?! She told me that the way I treated her was disgusting, and once again, I started to believe it. I was always doubting who I was. I thought I was a horrible person. She finally went to bed, and the next morning, it was like nothing had happened.

Writing that was such a release.

Sometimes, my mum would tell me that I needed help, and that I should see a counsellor. Being a teenager, I refused, and, of course, I wasn't going to agree. It was like she would tell me to go and get help and then expect me to book myself in. I was a teenager. I didn't know how to book a counselling appointment, nor did I want to. It would have done me the world of good to receive counselling, but she continued to attack me, telling me I needed help, without ever getting me the help I really did need. One day, my mother ended up taking me along to one of her own counselling appointments – so we could 'work on our relationship', she said. I didn't want to go, cracked it the whole drive there, as my mum tried to play the caring mother role. Once in the session, I felt like Mum and her counsellor/psychologist/whatever this lady was were straight-up attacking me. Mum played victim once again, and I was left looking and feeling like absolute shit. I was fifteen or sixteen when this happened, and this scared me away from seeking help for quite some time.

It was a hard battle with my mum, because the majority of the time, she was an awesome mum! She would tell me she loved me every day. She would say she was proud of me and would praise my achievements. She would cook amazing meals every night. She made a house a home. But as soon as the wines flowed, I was an abusive bitch of a daughter, brainwashed by her father. Apparently, I couldn't think for myself, and the sad part is, in the end, I actually couldn't think for myself, and my self-worth was so low, I didn't truly believe I could achieve anything I wanted in life. I had no faith in my abilities or faith in my thoughts being valid. I believed I was a bad person who didn't deserve anything good in life, and when good things did happen to me, I felt guilty, like I wasn't worthy. For example, I *hated* shopping when I was younger because I felt so guilty that money was being spent on me. I cracked it almost every time we went clothes shopping and these expeditions would end in tears.

One day, Dad made a comment that shook me to my core. He said to me, 'You're just like your mother.' I was instantly pissed off. I didn't want to be like my mother. At this stage of my life, I was still living in hate for things she had done. The last thing I wanted was to be like her. When Dad made this comment, I instantly associated negative things about her, probably because the comment didn't come from a place of love – it was voiced midway through a heated discussion. I started to question why this was so hurtful to me. Why did this little comment make me so wildly angry? Shouldn't people take it as a compliment to be told they are like their mother? This was a wake-up call that our relationship wasn't ideal.

After my parents split, Mum moved to the other side of Victoria, a few hours away. It felt like she was running away from her issues and us, her daughters. I don't see her very often now, mainly at Christmas and sometimes birthdays. I did really try with her for a while, tried to get her to stop drinking, and gave her money, but it was all too hard. You can't help someone who doesn't believe they have a problem, and it was hindering my mental health and I needed to put myself first. I feel my mother is a young soul on this earth, struggling in this earthly experience.

I had to be tough to get me through this. When this rigid façade becomes who you are and you act on autopilot, it is extremely hard to break down. Breaking this part of me down and feeling has been hard, but I am getting there through the writing of this book.

***

When a coping mechanism becomes who you are, it is difficult to unlearn it.

5

Kyanon

Ky is my younger sister. Ky is short for Kyanon, which I don't call her very often unless she has taken my favourite top or something. Growing up, Ky and I would argue, like sisters do. We would argue over clothes, food, the front seat in the car – everything you can imagine. One of her favourite phrases was, 'I know you are but what am I?' I laugh now thinking about those words and how angry I got because of them – it would always end in a fist fight! We didn't fight like little girls, pulling hair and slapping; we punched and booted the shit out of each other, like little ratbag boys would.

Ky was very close with Mum and I always felt like they would gang up on me during arguments, especially when Mum was on the wines – she always needed her little sidekick. If Dad was home, it seemed like it was Dad and me against Ky and Mum. Our relationship suffered from this for many years. I believed I hated my sister because of how angry I was the majority of the time.

I'm currently asking Ky questions, attempting to gain an understanding around her side of our relationship when we were younger. It was clear I struggled to get along with Mum, but why did that affect Ky and me so much? I'm shocked that we are close enough to go this deep within our childhood trauma together, very powerful stuff – I never thought we would get here.

I just asked Ky to write a little spill and this is what I got:

Mum would always divide us, like we were on teams. Me and Mum against Dad and Shay. Mum fed me comments like, 'Shay's a little bitch, isn't she, Ky? She and your father are just as bad as each other,' and she would remind me to never turn out like them. But growing up and moving out with Dad and Shay after my parents' separation made me realise that I actually didn't want to turn out like my mother. I thought Shay hated me my whole life because she was so angry and upset every day, but now I see why she was like that. It was because of Mum and the things she went through.

So great to know my own mother was telling my sister how much of a bad person she believed I was.

I wasn't nice to Ky and she wasn't nice to me. On the days that we were really close and getting along, I could sense Mum was threatened. Even though her words expressed happiness around the fact that we were getting along, I could just feel that she wasn't being truthful, and I don't know if she was even aware that she preferred us pitted against each other. It's like Mum needed her little sidekick by her side.

During my darkest periods, I was so unhappy, and I was bringing others down to make myself feel better. Ky would cop the brunt of it – no wonder she thought I hated her. Some days, I could be so nasty, picking at those around me. I took it to the next level when I would pick at people, saying hurtful things, beating them down. I would crush them. To put it plain and simple, I could be so nasty. Now, I wasn't always nasty; it was mainly during my younger years when I was emotionally drained. In my teenage years and early twenties, I turned to people-pleasing, wanting to make everyone happy and trying to only show the world my fun, happy self, no matter what was happening in my internal world. However, Ky would still cop the mean, unhappy side of me. My nasty ways usually popped up when I was tired, and my energy drained. It would just take over. I felt I couldn't stop, and after, I'd be left feeling extremely guilty for the sudden outburst and hurtful words I had conjured up. This was how I spoke to myself in my internal world, always picking, always focusing on the negative things about myself, beating myself down, and feeling low. I didn't have the knowledge, belief or tools to change this behaviour back then. It's true – if people are mean to you, or put you down, it's because they are not happy in their own lives. I was the one carrying the negative, lower vibrational vibes, and I blamed everyone else.

I needed to own up to the bullshit I told myself. I didn't know that the key to fixing this behaviour was through filling my own cup. When I started doing so, putting my growth before all else, my nasty behaviour quickly faded away, as I was looking after myself, loving myself and feeling good on the inside, so I had no need to tear others down to my level. I found myself lifting others up, encouraging others to love themselves the way I now do.

A while ago, I would not have ever admitted the nasty side of me that appeared in the past, as it triggered my ego, but I no longer identify with this. People do change, and I have mended myself. I feel this will be relatable for so many people. I was in survival mode, a slave to the mind; I have forgiven myself for the things I did and the person I was whilst I was purely trying to survive.

Ky and I deeply bonded after one night of pure shock. We stuck together like never before and built our relationship up from there. One day, Ky and I arrived home to find our mother lying face-down on the floor in the middle of the lounge room, passed out and lifeless. I assumed she had passed out from drinking too much, until she didn't get up when we tried to wake her, and for a brief moment, I thought she was dead. I made Ky leave the room and I shook her until she woke up. She was groggy, dazed and out of it, but alive. My mum had attempted to end her life that day, by taking some pills. Luckily, she survived, but from that point forward, Ky and I felt we could only truly rely on one another. We couldn't believe that Mum wanted to end her life and leave us. This one horrific day caused our bond to become unbreakable.

***

I was surviving, far from thriving.

6

Guilt Felt Like Home

I was living in a super low vibrational state the majority of the time. Throughout this book, you will notice I use the term 'vibration' or 'vibrational' often, and as I mentioned earlier, this refers to everything on this planet measuring at a certain vibrational frequency, e.g. lower emotions such as fear, guilt and shame vibrate at the lower end and that of enlightenment, which is our natural state but is conditioned out of us through society, is the highest level. Mid-higher vibrational states include acceptance, willingness, reason and love. Anything around acceptance, I consider an expanded state of awareness and anything below is contracted, living in the ego.

I was completely unaware and didn't know that the way I felt was something I would later be able to control. I thought most people felt how I did. I was an interesting case, though, and still am quite the oddball ... actually, I'll call it being unique! I also embrace my deepest self now! I'm all about my uniqueness! Anyway, I'd go to school each day, wanting so badly for the day to be done so I could get back to the comfort of my home. Once home, I would wish I could hide away anywhere that my mother wasn't. I was so sensitive to Mum and Dad's yelling, which was mostly triggered when the alcohol started flowing, it shook me to my core. Not that I let them see how badly it actually affected me. I felt my sister was tougher skinned in her younger days and had a much better relationship with my mum than I did. I feel it was because she couldn't see the damage the alcohol was doing to our family. I felt alone, because I was. I would hide away in my room or hide away on the couch under the blanket, keeping only my eyes and the top of my head visible so I could pretend to be very interested in whatever was on TV. When, really, my mind was running a loop of memories, past traumatic experiences and anything that brought about that homely feeling of guilt, shame and sadness. Because I lived in such a lower state, I felt the need to exaggerate my life to those around me. I made my life seem happy and more exciting than it actually was. I didn't want people to think I was unhappy.

It is so sad to think emotions that would usually be considered 'bad', and that feel bad, felt like home to me because they were familiar. I can now see why it can be so hard for people to change their lives. Familiar feels good, whether terrible or not. My mind all too often would easily confuse familiar for good, home, or 'meant to be'. Pushing out of my comfort zone is where I feel alive now.

***

Fighting my feelings caused the most suffering, not my actual feelings.

7

Leaving My Childhood Home

When my parents officially broke up, I was beyond relieved. That sounds so bad to say and I know break-ups are a horrible thing to go through, but the amount of anxiety and grief my parents caused Ky, me, and those closest to us is beyond me. Ky and I weren't allowed to see or even message our dad for the few months during their break-up due to an intervention order Mum placed against him. It was extremely hard. Living at home with my mum was a nightmare. I had so much anger towards her. We were constantly arguing. I was constantly getting my stuff thrown out of the house and being told to move out. I spent many nights at friends' places, and once I could finally see Dad again, I spent nights with him at Nanna's place. I was always moving around. Some days, I felt homeless, and I know that may sound silly, because I did have a home – I was just on the road so often during this time. I felt like Dad was all I had. This was all happening during year 12 for me, too. The pressure of VCE was too much with my unstable living situation, so I decided to step into the good old VCAL 'for dummies', as VCE students would call it. At this stage, I didn't care what I was doing at school. I was purely trying to survive and make it through each day. I thought about leaving school so many times, but I knew I needed to stay there, surrounding myself with my friends while I spent almost every day on the edge of tears. Throughout this period is when I would fantasise about moving out with Dad and Ky, finally escaping that toxic situation I called home. I craved a stable home life so badly – even typing this makes me want to cry.

Dad brought my fantasy of leaving that toxic situation to life. He had signed a lease for a rental property in Berwick. I cannot even explain how excited I was to escape. I don't know how much longer I would have survived in that environment. Ky decided to follow me and move in with Dad and me. We were both craving the emotional stability that we didn't receive. My sister and I were constantly drained, bags under our eyes and always on the edge of tears. The dreaded 'are you okay?' question often left me gasping for air at this stage of my life. Once moved, I found myself having to step up and support my sister, as she was very close with Mum and suddenly didn't have her around. I felt the weight of Ky's emotional well-being within my chest, even though this wasn't really mine to carry. I stepped up, dwindling away my own self in the process. Being in the situation of starting a whole new routine, learning how to cook and do all those household tasks my mum would usually do, which was way more work than I thought it would be, by the way, kept me busy enough that I could easily block out any healing that needed to take place within my own internal reality, pushing my depression and anxiety on the backburner.

Leaving my childhood home was more of a shock to the system than I ever thought it would be. I have always been a homebody and I would get excited every day to come home and veg out on the couch at night. I craved comfort and still do. Even when I was younger, I was happiest and most content at home in bed, wearing my fave dressing gown, sipping on tea, eating snacks and watching a flick, probably *Avatar* or *The Incredibles*. I kept it consistent because, remember, familiar feels like home. Even when my sister and I would have our cousins over, I guarantee, every damn time, I was the first in bed, and I was the oldest ... aren't the oldest meant to stay up the latest? Not my vibe. This goes hand in hand with my alone-time-loving self. There is just something I love about the feeling of home and comfort. I was beyond excited to have a new home, a fresh start for my dad, sister and me. I wasn't expecting to struggle with the whole creating something that 'felt like home' process but I did. It just didn't feel right, and I think it was because Mum wasn't around to make a homely space as she would. I constantly changed my room around, changed the house around, cleaned, moved things, lit candles – nothing quite felt like home. I missed the smell of the Emerald bush air, the smell of fireplaces burning in the hills during winter, that dusty smell older homes have, the candles my mum would burn, and my smelly childhood dog, Jessy. As I write, the tears in my eyes are building up from long-buried emotions, and are deeply healing my soul.

There was one major sign that moving was having a positive effect on me. When I was younger, I would talk, yell and scream at the top of my lungs in my sleep almost every night. Some of the most common things I would say were 'Get away from me,' 'Piss off,' 'Leave me alone,' 'Get off me,' and 'Fuck off.' I would never remember my dreams, or why I would say those things, and to be honest, I haven't really thought much about it until the idea popped into my head to put it in this book about five minutes ago. When I would stay at friends' places, I prayed I wouldn't scream in my sleep. I was so embarrassed. There were many times when I woke up my friends and their parents with my little episodes. Luckily, most people thought it was funny, and we laughed it off. I intuitively feel the words I was screaming out at night were everything I held in during the day; every emotion and word I held in throughout each day flowed out of my mouth while I slept. 'Flowed' is probably the wrong word – I would yell these words out at the top of my lungs. It would scare my mum. She honestly thought something was wrong with me and would come running into my room most nights. About three weeks after I moved away from my mum, my sleep screaming completely stopped. I still talk in my sleep occasionally, but no screaming. Writing this now has made it super clear as to why I was screaming in my sleep and it hurts me to realise this. I never wanted it to be the words I held back from my mother.

Still during this time, I was all about blocking out my emotions and didn't understand that I needed to feel hurt and sit with these emotions as they arose in order to be free of them. So I did what I did best, and I let it bottle up. I had a boy distracting me and some awesome friendships keeping me busy during this time, also keeping me out of this 'home' that didn't quite feel like 'home'. This boy, a few months after moving, became my first ever proper boyfriend. I put my entire focus on him. I was a loved-up eighteen-year-old. I admired him so much. I thought he was the coolest thing – it consumed me. I let many things bottle up and distract me from my trauma over the next couple of years until my awakening hit. I pushed the hurt further and further into my ego, not knowing that later I would have a real hard time when I started my shadow work journey, facing the darker thought processes that my mind held onto so tightly. Maybe if I had let the hurt consume me earlier, my awakening wouldn't have been such a major shock, but I was stubborn, and I believed not feeling was tough as fuck. I believed I could get through anything by turning my emotions off, but that slowly ate away at my humanity.

Dad changed once we moved into our Berwick home – less fiery, less triggered. We were all much happier around each other. I am so grateful for the life Dad has given Ky and me. He worked so hard to put a roof over our heads again and created that stable home we needed. He did so incredibly well holding us together during turmoil and I am so grateful.

This life-altering move pushed me closer but not over the edge into my awakened self just yet. My new boyfriend had my entire focus. There was no need to reflect on myself and how I was coping. I was occupied, placing my sense of self within another person.

I haven't really spoken widely about the experiences I'm relating in these chapters. I only told a select few about the darker things going on within my life at this time. Becoming vulnerable has always been a struggle for me. Now that I think about it – imagine when this book gets published. *Wow*. Something I know now is that people are going to perceive you through their own conditioning and their own ego. I am allowing myself to be free of judgements. This is my story. These are my soul messages.

Now, these next few chapters may make my life seem like a joke, and, far out, it was at times! Keep in mind there was time between these events. These are spaced over about five years, and there were so many good things that happened to me in-between, such as buying a couple of sick cars that I loved, graduating with my Double Diploma in Counselling and Community Services, finding my passion for design and scoring a full-time job for a local builder. I also got my little pug puppy, Phineus. He is the funniest dog in the world, full of character – one of the best things to ever happen to me. He is like my child. I partied with friends, went adventuring and have some incredible memories. However, I feel the happy times didn't trigger my awakening and this is what I'm here to write about. I am here to spill all my trauma, hurt, and grief out onto these pages, cracking me open into my new life, where I feel whole from within.

The pain is only temporary.

***

Buckle up, this is a wild ride.

8

Pulmonary Embolism

Things were finally starting to feel like home in our new routine. I felt like Ky and I were finding our feet after all the turmoil you go through as kids when your parents break up – you know, new home, new routine, all that jazz. Things with my boyfriend were great, I had some awesome friendships that were keeping me busy and I was living the life. I spent my time working at a car dealership in reception and bookkeeping, going to skid meets (I know, I was super cool), popping tyres on my VZ Commodore (yeah, I know, even cooler – sense the sarcasm – also, major tomboy), going out drinking and just all the usual young-people things. I was happy. Well, on the surface, at least. I still had all my shit buried.

Then, *bam!* The universe got me good; it was all too good to be true. I found when I wasn't living a soul-filled life that things kept going majorly wrong. One night whilst staying at my boyfriend's family home, I woke up at about 3 am with extreme chest pains. My chest felt like it had been stabbed all over, I couldn't breathe, and I was dripping in sweat. I had convinced myself in that moment that I was having a heart attack. *Good job, Shay. You probably sent yourself into shock, hahaha* (funny now, not then). I whacked my boyfriend awake, struggling to spit words out as he took one look at my face and sprinted out of the room to get his mum. His mum was a nurse at the hospital two minutes down the road. She took one look at me, lying in pain, dripping in sweat, and instantly told us to go to hospital! I got out of bed, struggling to put clothes on and made my way to the car. I was terrified, and the drive felt like forever. I had no idea what was wrong with me but I was convinced I was dying. By the time we got to the hospital, the pain had died down a bit but I was still struggling. When I got assessed, the nurse tried to tell me that I just had a chest infection. In that moment, I looked over to my partner with the expression of 'is she fucking joking?' on my face. I said to the nurse, 'This isn't a chest infection,' with a side of sass, and they took me straight in to be checked over. I don't know if it was because I stood my ground and said it wasn't a chest infection that they took me straight in, or if it was because my partner mentioned to the nurse that his mother was head of the emergency department – let's just say it was my firm hand.

As I just read over that previous paragraph, I was thinking – and I've been having this hovering thought – *Is this how you write a book? Am I doing this right?* Fuck that off. I am stopping that right now! I will not let my ego creep in and undermine me. I am a boss bitch. Anyway, you'll notice I get a little sidetracked, and I want you guys to be aware of me catching my ego creeping back in during writing, as this is me learning first-hand how to follow my soul and authentic truth. I got guided to write this book and my intuition is telling me that this is what I'm meant to do during this pandemic. I will not let my mind convince me otherwise.

After getting poked with needles, which is one of my greatest fears – oh, actually, I've got a funny story I will tell you. Stay tuned. Anyway, after getting poked with needs, getting x-rayed, and breathing in some metallic shit for a scan, they told me I had … *Insert Google definition* because I have no idea how to explain this:

Pulmonary Embolism: A condition in which one or more arteries in the lungs become blocked by a blood clot.

Most times, a pulmonary embolism is caused by blood clots that travel from the legs or, rarely, other parts of the body (deep vein thrombosis or DVT).

Symptoms include shortness of breath, chest pain and cough.

<u>*Prompt treatment to break up the clot greatly reduces the risk of death.*</u> *This can be done with blood thinners and drugs or procedures. Compression stockings and physical activity can help prevent clots from forming in the first place.*

Still to this day, the doctors haven't pinpointed what caused them, thinking maybe it was the contraceptive pill. Only a few years later, my sister had the same thing happen to her. As I write this, I am getting a vision of my sister waking up. Maybe she will have her awakening soon??? Oooh, I hope this book is done by then! Exciting stuff!

Anyway, back to it – the universe really threw a damn

curveball at me. I spent the next week in hospital, and this is where this funny story comes into play. Okay, so, as you know, I hate needles! Hate them! I faint and all sorts. There's something about the needle sucking stuff out of me or putting stuff into me that just doesn't sit well. There was a nurse that had started setting up to give me a needle one afternoon, but I was getting major student vibes, so I asked her as she filled this needle up, preparing to inject me, 'Are you even qualified?'

As she drew closer to jabbing my thigh with this huge blood-thinning, life-saving needle, she says confidently and proudly, 'I'm studying.'

And I said, with the look of terror on my face and a side of teenage-girl attitude, 'Are you even qualified, though?'

This student nurse looked over to the doctor in shock with a 'what do I do?' look on her face. The doctor jumped in, attempting to assist the student with me being the difficult patient I was, saying, 'She has given many needles and knows what she's doing.'

And I instantly said, 'She's not doing it. She's not even qualified.'

As this little conversation is happening, my boyfriend is standing on the other side of the curtain, listening and knowing about my fear and pissing himself laughing at the awkwardness that surrounded this poor student. If you are reading this, and you remember your days as a student nurse when some mean girl got on you about not being qualified, I want to sincerely apologise for my behaviour. Far out, I was a handful for that week of torture.

I thought once I left the hospital, the torture would be over.

Was I wrong! When I was in the hospital, I wasn't fully aware that I could have died and still could. This awareness hit me later while at home. I also wasn't aware that I would need to take life-saving, blood-thinning pills every day. These pills were trash. I couldn't drink with friends anymore. I bled from my gums and vagina at random times. I was constantly exhausted and had zero energy. I was covered in bruises, as when you're on blood thinners, you bruise very easily. I was whacked back down to a harsh reality that I didn't want to live in. I had the 'why me?' attitude going on. I would stay home when my friends would go out as I just didn't have the strength to go. You would think staying at home all this time would have triggered me to self-reflect, heal and wake up, but it didn't. Don't get me wrong. I definitely was more spiritually inclined, turning to cards and getting psychic readings occasionally, but it just wasn't the time to fully wake up yet.

These blot clots were a part of my life for the following eighteen months. During this time, they gifted me an immense appreciation for life and for perfect health as I craved it for myself once more, causing me to eat healthier, exercise more regularly, and care for my body more than ever before. At this time, I felt my prime years were taken away, which isn't true! I feel like my prime years have just started now! Walking this awakened path is like a whole new world. Re-reading that makes it sound like I'm fifty and I've had a midlife crisis, which, I guess, in a way, I have.

***

I will never take my health for granted again.

9

Rolling Hilux

Now, this next chapter I wasn't even going to write because the mere thought of it makes me bloody cringe. You should see my cringey face currently. *Argh*. See, this book is uncovering some deep shit I need to heal from.

It was summertime, a long weekend. I think it was Melbourne Cup weekend of 2016. My boyfriend, a group of our closest mates and I had all ventured up to Lakes Entrance in Victoria for a weekend away, camping at one of the guy's parents' farms. It was all going fine and dandy until the boys were all on the beers and we wanted to go into town. We needed two people to drive because we all wouldn't fit into one car. I volunteered to drive one of the guy's four-wheel drives as I hadn't drunk. We all hopped in and away we went. I was following our mates in front as I wasn't familiar with the area. My mate I was following had quite the lead foot and I struggled to keep up. He had taken a quick turn, and I quickly put on the brakes to make the turn also. Now, this is where things get hectic. This 1990's Toyota Hilux has a four-inch lift, thirty-five-inch mud tyres on it and these bad boys are known for being rolled without being super high off the ground. I hit this corner with a little too much speed, popping the car up onto two wheels. Everyone in the car screamed, as you would. I turned the wheel quickly, forcing us back down onto four wheels. At this stage, we would have been going no faster than 40 km per hour. However, the force of landing bounced us back up onto two wheels, tipping the car over onto my driver's side. It was all in slow motion for me. Like in a movie, we landed perfectly on the side of the road, as if I had done it on purpose. I looked around the car as we lay sidewards, the other passengers hanging above me screaming and crying. Everyone was okay, not a scratch on anyone. I felt a sigh of relief. I hadn't killed anyone, thank fuck. After booting out the windscreen, we all were free of the wreck that was once a pride and joy. I was so calm. I couldn't believe it. Maybe I was in shock. I was so embarrassed and ashamed; I couldn't believe it had happened. It was one of those 'please be a dream' moments. I had always prided myself on my driving, and now, look, I was defined as 'that girl who rolled a Hilux' and probably still am, if I'm honest with you. Writing this has killed my mood. I am feeling the emotions that I have buried for so long.

After this accident, I realised who my truest friends were – only a couple of my closest girlfriends checked in on me. I was the talk of the friendship group. Everyone was talking about me. It was all too much drama for me to handle, so I hid away at home for months, as I was too scared to face anyone. I was ashamed, embarrassed and I was so worried about how people viewed me. I couldn't function – honestly, I was a wreck. I knew I needed to move on from these friends as they weren't serving me or my growth, but this was a lesson I chose not to learn until I got whacked by the universe serval more times over the years. My anxiety was at the highest it had ever been before. My boyfriend supported me, which helped so much, but I still fell into depression. I let this trauma run on repeat through my mind for at least two years, every, single, day. I started seeing a counsellor, which really helped for a while. Being me, though, at this stage, I was still incredibly skilled at blocking out every traumatic experience as much as I could, letting it replay in my mind but not knowing how to feel and release the emotions around it. I was in a toxic state where my mind was controlling me.

Even today, people make jokes about me rolling the car, ruining someone's pride and joy, attempting to belittle me, attempting to find humour within a situation that some of these people weren't even there to witness. This is okay, though; everyone acts in mysterious ways. I'm a pro at bouncing jokes back and have healed enough to joke about it. I feel so much more at ease now in comparison to how I felt when I decided to take the leap and write this chapter. As much as I didn't want it to be, this was a huge part of my life, adding to the build-up. It's like a volcano – we're getting warmer, filling up more and more, getting closer and closer to the eruption of my awakening.

***

My mind was running a constant loop of painful memories.

10

I Love You

I've picked up my computer again after a few days' break. I feel each chapter is a different sudden strike of universal soul flow and I'm rolling with it! So here we go again – another doozy. Get ready for your heartstrings to be pulled.

This is another thing I'm putting into my book that would have made the old me break down in utter shame and embarrassment if shared with others a couple of years ago. I held this little secret very close to me, only venting to my closest and most trustworthy of friends. My own. MY. OWN. BOYFRIEND. Didn't love me! My boyfriend, two years into our relationship, didn't love me. As a twenty-year-old, I struggled with this, analysing every single thing I did, always thinking, *I wonder if this is why he doesn't love me?* I would compare myself to my friends around me. *Why do their boyfriends tell them they love them? Maybe I need to become more like my friends?* I was stuck in the egoic mind struggle and it hurt. This plagued my thoughts for months. I was so deep in the pit of ego that I couldn't even see a light out. I held onto the belief that one day he would love me – once I changed, once I became more this or more that.

Let's go back to the events that dug up this loveless discovery *insert laughing emoji*. My bestie and I would always chat about our relationships, as gals do. Before she and her boyfriend even started officially dating, he had told her he loved her. I found myself comparing my relationship to theirs. At this stage, I was just waiting around for him to say those magical words, as I thought that's how these things worked. You know, boy meets girl, girl and boy fall in love, boy tells girl he loves her and they live happily ever after. Fairy tales really drummed that into me, much like everything else within this society, shaping my state of consciousness and mind. Eighteen months into our relationship, I started thinking, maybe I'll say those magical little words, maybe the guy doesn't have to be the first one to say it, maybe me saying these words will give me the security of a long future together, that guarantee of lasting love – *HAHA*, I fucked up. One night we were lying in bed, spooning, my heart was pounding, palms were sweating, knees weak (just an absolute hot mess really *haha*). – by the way, I'm not covering pain with humour, as I am genuinely healed from this and am vastly grateful for this happening, but it's just hilarious remembering – and I tried to mutter those three little words.

I said my partner's name.

'Yes?' he says.

'Oh, don't worry,' I said.

This happened a few times until I finally muttered those torturous words, 'I love you.'

My heart was beating out of my damn chest. I couldn't believe I had said it! I desperately waited for his response. I clung to the blanket that was tightly gripped within my hand, brisk silence filled the air, nothing ... nothing ... nothing ... I got ignored. Nothing was said. My racing pounding heart shattered into a million pieces, not literally, but honestly, that's what it felt like. I received a delayed pat on the back, which felt like an 'it's okay, thanks, but I don't love you though' pat on the back. I felt unloved and unwanted because that's how I allowed myself to feel. My own boyfriend didn't love me, so I decided that there wasn't anything to love about myself.

There were a few occasions when my partner's dad brought up the fact that his son did not love me. He had obviously been talking to his parents about it, and I never knew what to say. What are you supposed to say in that situation? I guess there's not really a generic answer I could whip up in the moment. I would become so uncomfortable, nervous laughing and shrugging it off. I still don't understand why he felt the need to bring this up. Surely, he would have known this would hurt me. But, as I did, I blocked it out, and continued trying to think positive.

Eventually, he did say those three little words to me, but they didn't live up to the hype. They were just words, and saying them didn't show me the love I wanted so badly. This stage of my life I look back on now and I feel sorry for past me. I let three little words, or lack of, affect everything I did – the way I dressed and how I acted – all because I was hoping if I became a certain person, my boyfriend may love me. How did I have such a lack of confidence in myself and who I was? I guess I didn't really know who I was. How did I just live in this pain, acting like nothing was wrong? When I say pain, I'm not necessarily talking about the relationship wholly as past pain, I am referring to past me, my past attitudes towards myself and my beliefs that kept me trapped within a small box, crippling my earthly experience.

***

I was searching for love outside of myself.

11

Ashamed

My fear of being vulnerable prevented me from speaking up about something that I let eat away at me for far too long. I am so damn ready for this to be spoken about openly. I am so ready for this weight to be lifted off my subconscious. To all my close family and friends, I hope this chapter paints a clear picture as to why I suffered in silence. I also hope this can help other women who have been in a similar position to speak up. This is nothing to be ashamed of. This is natural! Lean on the people around you – friends and family, if you can. There are people who want nothing more than to support you. If you don't feel comfortable talking to your friends and family, reach out to an expert. Please don't go through this alone.

This all started one day when I went to hospital because I had slight chest pain. Nothing serious – I just thought I had better get it checked out to make sure my blood clots hadn't returned. A few days prior to this, my partner and I had a few rough nights. We weren't the happiest with one another, so I didn't tell him I'd gone to the hospital until I had left and got the all-clear on the blood clot front. While at the hospital, they took blood and did all the usual tests they do. Obviously, when they take blood, they also check to see if you're pregnant. So once the test results came back, one of the male doctors came and sat down next to my bed. I knew straight away something was up, thinking, *Oh no, these damn clots are back again.*

He says to me in the nicest, softest, most gentle voice, 'Shaylyn, the blood test has come back showing that you're pregnant.'

I said, 'What? How? I'm on the pill.'

My mind instantly shot back to a couple of months prior when we were camping, where I thought I had missed a day or two taking the pill. I burst out into tears, and the doctor asked if there was anyone he could call for me. In that moment, I instantly thought, *No one can know.* So I said, 'No, thank you. It's okay.' The doctor explained to me my options and, in a panic, I asked if they could terminate the pregnancy right there and then. I was terrified of people finding out and I knew I couldn't properly care for a baby at this point in my life. I was only twenty years old, still living at home. The doctor explained that I needed to go to my GP and get a referral for an abortion clinic. I jumped out of the hospital bed. My mind was running a million miles an hour. I wanted so badly to call my partner crying, but I knew he wouldn't take the news well at all and I thought this was something better told in person. I got in my car and drove straight to my family doctors' clinic thirty minutes away. I ensured I didn't see my usual family doctor as I was so embarrassed and ashamed to be pregnant. But in saying that, even though I knew to my core that now was not the right time for me to have a baby and that I wouldn't be able to support a child properly, I had this overwhelming feeling that I needed to care for myself and this baby. It was like nothing I had ever felt before. The emotion was strong and I felt it deep within my core. It confused me as I knew I wasn't having the baby, yet it was a truly beautiful, natural thing to feel.

After seeing a GP I got a referral for an abortion clinic. I called and booked in to see them in seven days, which felt like a lifetime away but it was the soonest appointment they had available. That night, I tried to tell my partner of the horrid day I had. I tried to tell him I was pregnant. I was still processing this myself and didn't fully believe it. I tried to spit those damn words out. I was an absolute hot mess of a human once again, shaking, sweating, the whole deal *haha*! Okay, I'll stop. This is a serious time. I guess this is the great thing about unobservant boyfriends – he had no idea there was anything wrong with me. The next night, we took Phineus for a walk. I tried to tell him again, but the words wouldn't come out. I was terrified of his reaction. I was ashamed in myself that I had let this happen and it was just all too much. The same thing happened for the next couple of nights. I still hadn't told him, and he still had no idea that there was anything wrong with me.

The day before I had my appointment at the abortion clinic, I went to the toilet in the morning for my good old morning wizzle. Something felt off. I looked down at the toilet bowl. Blood was pouring out of me. It was like nothing I'd ever experienced before. I instantly felt a huge sense of relief come over me, thinking I had most likely lost the baby, which feels so bad to write. I would never hope for this or wish this upon anyone. It's a heart-wrenching experience. But during this time, a baby was not an option for me. I called my GP and spoke to him about what was happening, and he said it was most likely I was having a miscarriage, but urged me to still go to the abortion clinic the following day to have things checked over and ensure I didn't need any further assistance.

So that night, I grew the balls to tell my partner about what had been going on the past week and release those cringy words: 'I'm pregnant.' We were watching a movie in bed. I rolled over to him and said, 'I need to tell you something.' His face was not impressed and I don't think he quite knew what I was about to say. The following words came out so damn quickly I forgot to breathe. 'When I went to the hospital last week, they told me that I was pregnant, and I've booked an appointment for tomorrow. But then this morning, I had blood coming out, and they think I've lost the baby, so I still have to go to the abortion clinic tomorrow in case they need to assist.' The look on his face in this moment was one of pure shock. I could tell he was angry, confused and stunned, all at the same time. I could barely look at him. He asked me how this happened as I was on the pill and all the usual questions, as you can imagine. He also made it very clear that no one could know. I agreed because I was so ashamed, and, at the time, thought that was for the best – geez, I was wrong. The next day, I was hoping my partner would come with me to the clinic, but I knew that wasn't going to happen and I was wishing for too much. I understand we all have our own ways of coping with things and his was to avoid the situation.

As I drove to the clinic the next morning, hunching over in my seat and clenching the steering wheel whilst the worst cramps of my life hit my body, I found myself feeling more alone than I ever had in my entire life, but I also had this extreme feeling of love and care, like a sense of being at one with myself radiating from within. I still can't fully describe this feeling but it was truly beautiful. I hope when I'm pregnant in the future, I get to feel this all over again. I found myself reaching for my phone to call my closest friend, Jacqui. All I wanted to do was cry to her, tell her everything, get her to come and see me, and if I had called her, there's no doubt in my mind that she would have been there within the hour – she's my angel on earth – but I threw my phone down on the passenger seat, and stayed strong, alone.

Once I arrived at the clinic, I was questioned about why I was there alone, and I was also made aware that if I needed the procedure, I wouldn't be able to drive home after. The nurse urged me to contact a friend or partner to come and support me, but I said I couldn't. I broke down to this nurse. I couldn't hold the tears in. I was scared and felt so alone. After speaking to the nurse for quite some time, we had decided that patient transport would be the best option if the procedure went ahead. This was going to be one expensive after-abortion Uber. They prepped me for an ultrasound to see if I had lost the baby. I had – I was relieved, upset and filled with guilt for the women who want nothing more than to have a child. The ultrasound nurse informed me that I would continue to pass blood, experience cramping, and, at some point, I may even see the foetus. Before I left the clinic, I went down to see the nurse that listened to me cry for an hour before the ultrasound. I thanked her for being so understanding and helping me with other options transport-wise. She made the whole time less shitty; she's another angel on Earth. I wish I could thank her again.

Driving home from the clinic is when it all hit me super hard, like a wave of emotions. I was pregnant – me, myself and I, pregnant?! Wtf! Then another wave hit me. I had lost the baby. One hundred thoughts and questions ran through my mind. *Can I even have kids?* I was scream-crying – you know when you're crying so hard, it's like you're screaming and howling? Yeah, that was me in my car on the drive home, clenching the steering wheel and hunching over once again, this time not because of cramps. I never really put much thought into having children before this moment, and now I was wondering if this was even a possibility for me. I told myself I most likely lost the baby due to the extreme stress and pressure I put on myself. But the one thought that consumed my mind and ate away at me was that my own boyfriend wasn't there to support me! The one person who is meant to have your back wasn't there for me and I was driving home all alone. I should have taken this as a sign, or a lesson or something, but I just let it be. I told myself that this was just his way of coping. I told myself that he would be there to support me that night after TAFE.

Once home, I waited for my partner to finish TAFE and come straight over. I was a wreck but had to act normal around my sister and dad. The hours passed, and my boyfriend still hadn't got home. I thought maybe he had gotten stuck in traffic.

I didn't want to annoy him by calling, so I just patiently waited. Another hour passed and I started to worry. I messaged him, asking where he was. He said he was with the boys and he would be home soon. Once again, I started crying. I was an emotional wreck. All I wanted was someone to cuddle. I just needed someone there. I couldn't believe he thought seeing the boys was more important than seeing if your god damn girlfriend is okay after having a miscarriage and spending the day at an abortion clinic alone. But I told myself it was his way of coping, and he would be over soon enough. He ended up getting home at 9:30 pm. Keep in mind, I'm a nanna – remember 9:30 pm is past my bedtime. He walked into my room and I instantly started crying.

'I really needed you today,' I said as I lay curled up in a ball in bed. He didn't really give me a response. He hopped into bed and gave me a cuddle. I was so happy he was there, I started to vent about my day, but I could feel he didn't want to know about it. So, I mentioned to him again that I really needed him and staying out with the boys didn't seem to me like it was the right thing to do.

He angrily rolled over away from me to be facing the wall and went to sleep. He emotionally manipulated me, time and time again, and I kept making excuses for it in my mind. I also wasn't fully aware that I was being manipulated at this point, so that didn't really help me. I was blind to it. That night, I cried myself to sleep, thinking maybe tomorrow (which was Thursday) we would talk about it.

I didn't see my boyfriend again until Monday night. He went away with the boys for the weekend and didn't check in on me once. I waited for a text or call, but nothing. I ended up buying a sewing machine and turned my focus to making swimwear for the entire weekend as a way to keep myself occupied (swimwear was another failed business venture of mine, *haha*). I wish he knew the hurt and pain I felt during that weekend. The peak of this shitty weekend happened Saturday at around midday. I was home alone, curled up in a ball on the shower floor, crying in pain; a pool of watered-down blood surrounded me. I didn't know you could bleed this much and survive. This is when I birthed the foetus. I would have been about nine to ten weeks at this stage. This was the shock of my life. I wasn't 100% sure whether it was my baby or gunk until I whipped out my phone and searched online. But there it was. It was real. This was happening. I think this was the longest shower of my life. I sat there for at least two hours. I even think the water went cold for a solid twenty minutes before I got up off the floor and turned the taps off. I was numb.

Once my boyfriend arrived home from his little boys' trip, we continued life as normal, as if this whole little situation didn't happen. On rare occasions, I would try to bring it up, as I felt I needed to talk about it. I was feeling so alone even a few months on. It was constantly on my mind, as much as I tried to block it out. I beat myself up over forgetting the pill and falling pregnant for months. I was so hard on myself for my forgetfulness. I had this massive secret, a painful, life-changing event that no one knew anything about hanging over me, and this made me question my relationship every single day from that point forward. If I could not speak to the person closest to me, what was the point? Not a day went by that I didn't think about leaving my partner. Even on the best days, it was always sitting in the back of my mind, and I guess I always knew deep down I wasn't meant to be with him forever – you know, that little doozy we call 'inner knowing'. I would still attempt to plan our future and push for him to also, but I never got what I hoped – it never really felt right – but I just told myself that it was because we were young. I was never a part of his future plans when he spoke about them either. His future plans always revolved around materialistic things, like cars, expensive homes, motorbikes and boats – all big dreams, which is awesome! I'm all about dreaming big, but I also include the things that truly matter within my big future dreams, like love, family, friends, helping others, a home and jet skis.

I never really felt I got much closure after my miscarriage until about two years later. I booked in to have my first ever reiki session with a lovely lady named Rebecca. After the reiki was complete, Rebecca explained to me how she was shown an image of the sun, but intuitively felt it meant son, young boy, my ray of sunshine, a sense of a young boy with me, by my side, and I instantly knew this was my baby. I could feel it. I feel him in my presence every now and then. It's hard to describe, but it feels like love. This was my closure.

***

Vulnerability is my gift.

12

The Crumbling

Over the years, I have dealt with unbearable times, but I held onto the belief that everything was happening for a reason. Yes, I know my life wasn't the worst in the world and I know others have it much worse than I did, but far out! I wanted to give up! I'd had enough! I was in that victim mentality, always asking, *Why is this happening to me?* I had no idea that our beliefs create our reality and I was throwing petrol on the fire with my growth-hindering thoughts.

I channelled all my energy and focus from these bad experiences into one goal and I achieved it! At the age of twenty-one, I bought an investment property! Ever since I was about thirteen years old, I wanted to buy an investment property. I felt that this would secure my future, and being a Cancer, I so deeply craved the stability I didn't have when I was growing up. In my mind, I gave an investment property the meaning of security for my future self and my future family. I believed an investment property ensured that I would be able to afford to create the home I wanted when I was older. I also hoped it would make my boyfriend proud. I hoped he would finally love me, as he put such high value around financial achievements. All I wanted was for him to be proud of me, and I thought that maybe after buying a house, I would be worthy of his love, which sounds absolutely ridiculous now, but this is how my mind would think in the past.

I had been watching the property market for a while and I had put a deposit on a block of land. Then I started getting signs to sell the land and look at buying established. You wouldn't believe it – my stars aligned. After being guided to look at a certain place, having that little intuitive feel, and synchronicities, the girls planned a weekend away literally ten minutes down the road from this suburb. Two days before our trip, the perfect, little, white, weatherboard, three-bedroom, one-bathroom home came up for sale. *THANKS, UNIVERSE.* The day we were leaving to go on our little getaway, I left a little earlier to check out this house. It was perfect. I put in an offer that day. Seven days later, I had paid the deposit and forty-five days later, the house was mine. It was all so easy, like it was meant to be, and I was beyond excited! In my mind, this was the greatest achievement I could attain for myself at my age! I was pumped! So proud of myself! Prouder than I had ever been!

My excitement quickly diminished. I could sense my partner at the time wasn't very happy about it and didn't feed in on my excitement, even though his words were expressing happiness for me. My damn intuition is too strong and I could feel it in my chest that he wasn't happy at all. Verbally, he always supported my dreams, but energy-wise, I could feel his lack of support and doubt around everything I did, and I couldn't seem to shake it no matter how hard I tried. I would focus on his encouraging words, doubting and continually suppressing my intuitive senses, but the feels took over. The energy showing me that he wasn't super proud of me like I had hoped, crushed me; I couldn't work out why he wasn't jumping for joy and showing me the love, support and happiness I so deeply craved. I would frequently doubt my intuition and place my trust in his misleading words. I was searching for everything outside of myself.

This is when the universe throws a giant LOL at me! Seriously, I'm laughing just thinking about it! ONE month after I had bought my first investment property, just one month after – and ONE MONTH before I'm meant to embark on a life-changing European holiday that every twenty-one-year-old chick dreams of – I GET MADE REDUNDANT! I! GET! MADE! REDUNDANT! See what I mean? What a bloody joke! My life came tumbling back down! Who said waking up is meant to be easy?! This is when I got cracked open into my spiritual awakening. I was waking up, but I was completely unaware. This is *my reality of spirituality*!

Getting made redundant sent me into a downward spiral, spinning with stress and anxiety, to the point where I made myself physically ill. My dad was a great support at this time, telling me, 'It's just money. Go travel. Everything will work out once you're back home.' I was lucky I had enough savings to go on this life-changing trip. This wasn't the typical 'life-changing' trip as many young people experience it. For example, I did get drunk and party like never before in beautiful cities with incredible people, but this trip made me really question what I wanted out of life. It made me see that the job I got made redundant from wasn't serving me at all and actually was a huge part of my unhappiness. During this trip, I started to question absolutely everything in my life. I wanted more. I wanted to do more, see more, feel more, become more!

This trip involved travelling with a group, which wasn't for me. I crave alone time and my empath self struggled hard. Oh, the things we do for love. We spent the majority of time on a bus, and I couldn't help but be constantly drawn to entrepreneurs and the whole self-employment scene whilst flicking on my phone. I was flooded with inspiration; the universe was telling me something. I always had an inner knowing that I would one day work for myself. However, this holiday and seemingly endless bus time had given me the opportunity to put some real thought into it. I was set on creating my ideal future and ideal life. I didn't want to work the nine to five. I was destined for more. I visualised my dream life every time I got back on that damn bus. I found myself so excited to get home to pursue this new life for myself.

Once home, the reality of having no money hit me. I fell into a deep depression. I worried about how I would pay my bills, keep my little nest-egg investment and purely survive. Each day would get worse and worse. Even writing about this now is bringing up old wounds that I didn't realise were still this raw. My dad was still an incredible support. Continually telling me not to worry about money. 'You will get a job when the time's right.' I knew he was right. However, being in such a low vibration state, nothing that was said to me sunk in. I could not think clearly. My mind was my own worst enemy. In the midst of my 'lostness', I found myself looking to spiritual practices, spiritual influencers and reiki for some guidance and the emotional peace I so deeply craved. I felt like I was opening a whole new part of myself. I filled my room with crystals, and burnt sage almost every day, hoping to gain some clarity in my life. I would flick through my oracle cards over five times a day, hoping for some clear guidance and answers. I was lost within my destructive mind. I didn't feel like I was living my own life. I wanted the cards to tell me what I should do next. I would frequently pull similar cards: 'energy work', 'counsel others', 'entrepreneur', 'creative project'. This lasted for months. I was stuck in a low place and I couldn't see out of it. I was determined to find my life's purpose and I put my entire focus on this, but my self-doubt was blocking me.

I always felt that I had a greater purpose on this earth. The 9 am to 5 pm lifestyle always seemed so unrealistic to me. In fact, I couldn't even wrap my head around it – how is that life? Working five days to have two days off? WTF? I also hated the idea of working my ass off and draining myself to give another the financial freedom I wanted and deserved! Plus, always feeling this deeper purpose calling me was something I couldn't ignore. I knew I needed to push past this societal structure and choose a career that others most likely wouldn't see as a career. I could just feel it deep within me. I battled with this for years, forcing myself into courses, convincing myself that this next thing was my purpose. I put up so much resistance around finding my life's purpose that I prevented it from coming in.

I was extremely lost and on the hunt for my purpose in life and security. The more I chased security, the further away it was, and the greater insecurity I felt. I was unhappy, stressed, anxious and depressed, searching for more. This was my spiritual awakening cracking me open. I was on the hunt for what set my soul on fire. I felt if I found my life's purpose, this would give me a sense of identity and I would no longer be lost. But it was the shift out of identity I needed.

***

The more I craved security, the more insecurity I felt.

13

Lost and Searching for My Purpose

Over the next two years, I battled through my awakening, unaware, unhappy and struggling. I went through these little phases of 'life-purpose excitement', I'll call them. Struggling to find my reason for living, I knew I had a greater purpose and I was set on finding it. I'd feel like I'd found what I was meant to be doing in this world, imagining living the life of freedom I craved, and for a brief moment, I no longer felt lost. I would start out on a high, a rush of excitement! Thinking, *Yes! This is what I'm meant to do!* Now, when I say a rush of excitement, I mean, I would let this little idea take over. I would research, plot and visualise. Immediately, I would start planning my new life within my head, how I thought I wanted it to be, dropping my ideas to those around me, trying to convince them that this was a great idea and that I was so passionate about it. Who was I really trying to convince, though? Myself! I knew I wasn't passionate about these bullshit money-making schemes that never made me money! But I was passionate about finding my purpose, hoping, praying and begging that the next thing was it! I was desperately searching but feeling more lost with every failed attempt.

I was working for a builder before I was made redundant. I have a passion for building and design and could see myself helping and guiding people through their home personalisation and selection process. After sitting on the thought during my Contiki trip and for months after, KYLYN Design was born. I subcontracted to various new-home builders, taking their clients through their home personalisation and selection process, everything from façade colours and finishes to tap fittings. At the start, I was so passionate about this little business of mine, picturing myself successful and living the dream, I convinced myself this was my life's purpose, and I was putting so much effort into getting this business going, I couldn't work out why I'd always come to roadblocks. Even whilst living in the excitement of starting a new business, I still craved a more spiritual path. However, I couldn't see how I would survive living that hippie life and I couldn't see being spiritual as a 'career'. So, I created this vision in my head of a successful design business. I soon lost that spark as I struggled to work with people designing their homes. It was repetitive, and I rarely got the opportunity to work on designs that I loved. I had been making some income but not enough to live out my wildest dreams. It just wasn't in alignment with me, so it wasn't flowing as easily as it should. Needing money once again, I set off on the hunt for a part-time job. That way, I could keep this design business in the works, whilst making some more cash, so then maybe I could start living my dream of building my own home and moving out. I would receive signs and intuitive hits pushing me towards the spiritual life I longed for but couldn't imagine how I would make it a reality, so I didn't.

Still pushing for building design to be my purpose in life, I thought studying would bring me closer to my goals, giving me a greater skillset to invite in more work. I had convinced myself that I wanted to study a Diploma of Building Design (architectural). I do love building design and architecture, plus this would have given me the knowledge to grow my business, but it just wasn't in alignment with me. Of course, I continued to resist, though, pushing back with my ego and creating that dream within my mind of the life I thought I wanted with my partner at the time. So I signed up for this course, and on my first day, everything that could have possibly gone wrong went wrong. There was a crash on the freeway so I was late. I couldn't find a car park because I was late. I got a parking ticket. My laptop wasn't working. I couldn't find the classroom because they had moved. It was all turning to shit. A few weeks into the course, I realised and accepted the fact that it wasn't for me – this was actually during a meditation that one of the teachers would make us do every lesson, which I thought was incredible. I would look forward to her classes just for these beautiful little guided meditations she would run us through. On the spur of the moment, after walking out of that class, I unenrolled in the car park as I was leaving that day, without talking to my dad or my partner. I just swiftly unenrolled with one simple email. It felt so good.

See how spirituality somehow always found me when I needed it most? How rare is it that a teacher takes a class through a guided meditation each lesson, and how crazy is it that I was placed in her class out of all the teachers at this TAFE? Everything happens for a reason. On the drive home, I thought about what other courses I could do now that I had thrown this plan down the drain, and I decided that maybe another interior design course was the plan of action. Once again, I was guiding myself with my ego mind, not tuning into my soul and what my true purpose was. I was putting so much pressure on myself to study again so I could have an amazing business. Off I went again, driven by my ego and the idea of the life I wanted painted within my mind. I started a higher education Diploma of Interior Design and Decoration, a great course for upskilling KYLYN Design. I lasted one trimester, failing a subject, and dropped out. *What next?* I thought. Obviously studying design wasn't the way to go.

I had suffered anxiety most of my life, and depression kicked in during my teen years, but this was all heightened and more intense than ever before after being made redundant, searching for my purpose and starting a mediocre business. I felt like my life was just a series of lows. I was constantly battling to create income from my severely out-of-alignment business and wanted to just give up. Anxiety and depression were things I battled with quietly, seeing a counsellor every now and then when I couldn't pull myself out of that hole alone and needed a professional helping hand up, especially during the early days of my awakening when I was more lost than ever before and had no idea how to fix myself. I thought this was the effects of my tough-girl mindset, blocking out my feelings and letting everything I had bottled up over the years leak out of me through anxious episodes and depressive states, and maybe it was. However, now I see the heightened anxiety and depression were a part of my awakening and the transformative shifts of energy I was having that I was completely unaware of.

My spiritual awakening was brutal at this stage. I was still lost as fuck, and completely unaware of the huge transformation I was about to uncover that would finally explain my vast 'lostness'.

***

Hunting for my purpose in life only caused it to run away.

Little Life Update

I just had a reiki appointment with my reiki practitioner, Rebecca. During the session, she mentioned to me that she was shown a vision of me walking along the beach, leaving a feather with each step I took. I was leaving my own unique mark on this world, living a life of impact. I feel this book is my own unique imprint on this world.

14

The Relationship that Broke Me

Now, firstly, this relationship didn't break me because of the person I was with; this relationship broke me because of my toxic beliefs, traits and the way I treated myself within my internal world, which reflected straight back into my reality. Our beliefs truly do create our reality. However, at this stage, I was completely unaware of this universal truth and previously had the mindset of 'why is this happening to me?' I am very grateful for this relationship now. It changed me, breaking down my façade and forcing me to turn inward to my spiritual awakening.

We met during high school and got together not long after school ended. We were eighteen at the time and I had just started my new life living with Dad and Ky. I was so infatuated with the idea of having an actual boyfriend that I was in complete denial about how this relationship actually made me feel. I would always try to focus on the good things, as I felt guilty about even having a thought around not being happy, and I believed I should be happy. We had great friends. We had a great lifestyle – camping, four-wheel driving, going to festivals, going on a few amazing holidays. We were living the early twenties' good life. However, emotionally, I was all over the place. It was unhealthy. I struggled to see my worth outside of this relationship, and within the relationship, I couldn't establish healthy boundaries for myself. I feared his rejection, which tended to happen often as we would make plans and I would be left waiting for him to rock up hours later, if he actually did end up rocking up. I needed his approval for everything I did, not because he said I needed his approval but because I just wanted to make him happy. My taste in things was entirely shaped around what I believed he would like. I never thought about what I truly wanted. What I liked felt so foreign and unimportant. I always felt responsible for how he was feeling, and put his emotions above my own, sacrificing myself along the way. The majority of the time, I would keep quiet around things I wanted to speak about to avoid arguments, until the build-up got too much and I'd crack, becoming either super-reactive or defensive once he peeped up. He would often speak to me terribly in front of our friends, and I would make excuses for his behaviour. That is when I felt super uncomfortable within myself, as I could see that it was wrong, but I went against my instincts. I was afraid to speak my truth, as I never felt heard, or felt my truth wasn't valid because he didn't agree with it. I thought this was okay. I believed this was 'normal'. I believed this was just how things were meant to be, continually convincing myself that I had no reason to be unhappy and that I just needed to focus on the good more. I would tell myself to stop being negative.

I was difficult to be with. I was closed off, scared to open myself up, overcompensatingly independent due to being let down so much when I was younger. I had terrible communication skills. I expected him to be able to read my mind when I couldn't even read it myself. I was not in touch with my feelings. I was moody at times, drowning in childhood trauma and wounds that I was yet to deal with. I didn't love myself and it all affected us far more than I thought it did. Not only did I struggle to open up in this relationship due to fear around his fiery reactions, but I also feared opening up due to hurt from my upbringing. I felt I needed to heal but I just didn't know where to start. It felt all too overwhelming, so I blocked it out, putting more and more strain on our relationship, mainly focusing on his well-being as opposed to my own. I put this person on such a high pedestal. Everything in my life revolved around him. I always tiptoed around, ensuring he was experiencing the best life possible with me. I was attached and co-dependent, although I'd never let the world see that. I wanted to keep my carefree persona. I wanted to be the cool, easy-going girlfriend that was just happy going with the flow, which, in turn, was allowing myself to be walked all over in the process. I gave myself value based on how good a girlfriend I was, how little fights I started and how good I was at keeping the peace – it was extremely toxic. This was my identity, and for a while, I struggled with a loss of identity within many relationships in my life, always trying to become what I thought another person needed or wanted – people-pleasing at its absolute finest.

I feel due to the timing of this person coming into my life, I avoided the healing I needed from my childhood. This relationship had started to fly as soon as I moved out of my childhood home. I leant on him by occupying myself and keeping busy in every spare moment I had, after work and study. I could never really speak to this boyfriend about any of my troubles in-depth, so I didn't, and I put it down to the fact that he was young. But thinking back now, our communication skills were absolute trash. Nothing was ever communicated properly, as I struggled to speak up, and for him, I was last option during the early days of our relationship. Actually, I was last priority until we broke up. (Classic, hey? That's always the way.) But this is because that was how I treated myself. This was all a part of my internal world reflecting back to me. These patterns that played out during our relationship were patterns and lessons I needed to learn from and had been played out whilst living with my mum. I was repeating a pattern, repeating a soul lesson, and I wasn't learning – I was completely unaware. I continued to use my 'skills' of blocking out emotions, as I thought this was the correct thing to do. I was extremely out of alignment and I don't know how I lived with myself.

I felt like feeling and expressing any form of lower emotion was negative whilst in this relationship, and eventually when I did start to try to voice how I felt, trying to create change within myself and no longer wanting to suppress my emotions, I was labelled 'negative'. He gave me this label because I would frequently say that I wanted to stay away from negative people and situations within my life, so this would get thrown back on me, making me feel like I was becoming the thing I wanted to avoid. I'd feel so uncomfortable within myself when this would occur. I truly started believing I was being negative, just because I felt the need to speak up about how I was feeling. Most of the time, the way I was feeling was due to his actions, so it makes so much sense to me now why he would use this as an opportunity to flip it back on me. There was no space for expression when it hurt his ego or mine, which seemed to be often. I felt I was constantly battling to keep a happy persona because I didn't want to be a negative person. He would frequently complain about every little thing in life and would love to sit in an angry state. This was hard to block out, especially because I was so sensitive to energy. I didn't allow myself to see that he was a negative person because he always made out like it was me – *classic*. I focused on the positives in our relationship, but never allowed myself to actually feel any of this positive energy.

It took me over a year to realise that my own boyfriend was jealous of me buying a house. He hadn't achieved his goal of buying a house just yet, so he couldn't be happy for me. Jealously ruled him. Once I realised this, I started to notice that almost everything he did was to be 'better' than someone, or to own something that was 'better'. I never realised before because I always looked at him in a positive light and wanted to see the best in him. Then I realised he was always competing with me too. Everything I did, he had to one-up me, and was never actually happy for me. My awakening was revealing shadows in my life. The more I noticed this, the more I started to not like the person he was and the more I started to not like the person I was when I was around him. This competitive energy rubbed off on me. I was found constantly trying to be more, never accepting and being grateful for what I had. This is when I started to accept my unhappiness and the truth about how I really felt in this relationship, and how this wasn't the type of love I wanted. I was disappearing into the person I loved, spending my time pouring myself into a relationship that I thought I wanted.

Even when he was the most loving and caring boyfriend in the world, I didn't allow this into my space. I didn't believe it and therefore I couldn't appreciate it. I didn't know how to accept love or be vulnerable because of the beliefs and walls I placed around myself. My understanding grows the more I write; the awareness creates peace. This is a beautiful and powerful part of my story.

***

My healing started as soon as I stopped pretending I wasn't hurting.

15

Lion's Gate Portal

Over the past couple of weeks, I have seen a lot of posts and images floating around online about the 'lion's gate portal'. I had never heard of this before and, naturally, my spiritual self was intrigued. I told myself I would investigate it more, but I just kept putting it off, thinking, *I'll get to it*. I had seen on someone's post that this lion's gate energy is at its peak on the 8th of August each year. I had planned to do some journaling on this date to tune in to this universal energy, as these online posts were suggesting.

Firstly, what is the lion's gate portal? The star Sirius rises, which becomes visible in the eastern sky on or around 8/8 each year. It aligns with the powerful summer Sun in Leo, and the numerological symbolism of the number 8. All these factors carry majorly auspicious symbolism and work together to make August 8th a particularly lucky day for manifesting success and turning your dreams into reality!!! I can see it! Me, a published author, travelling around the world, living in my dream home, healing and connecting with others! Anyway! So, if you're into setting intentions or connecting with cosmic energy like I am, you don't want to miss this opportunity. Aim high as hell! Here I was yesterday dreaming and manifesting this book just getting published. Here I am today, envisioning and tapping into this cosmic energy, believing and truly feeling that this book will give me the abundance to live my dream life, but also the platform for me to connect and heal others, as my soul deeply craves; P.S. I also want a jet ski! Wait, wait! Aim higher, Shay! I want twenty jet skis for all my friends and family! Wait! Aim higher again! I'M GOING TO OWN A WHOLE DAMN TROPICAL ISLAND! Where I will run retreats and help thousands of people! Do you get me now?! This is a time to step up and manifest your wildest dreams! I can picture myself in the future looking back on this little chapter and laughing, as I lie in the backyard of my dream home sipping an iced chai latte made by my soul-mate hubby, who will be hilarious and hot as hell, by the way.

Anyway, back to my current reality. Today is the 8th of August. Today is the day. Earlier this morning, I had mentioned to my soul sister, Millie, that it's lion's gate portal's peak today. At this stage, I still didn't know much about it! I just had the strongest sense that we needed to tune in to this energy to shift ourselves to the next level in life, as we both have a higher purpose. Anything we have been aiming for should come to fruition if we take advantage of this energy that will be hanging around until the 12th of August. I got so excited and pumped up!

I could feel this energy calling me and circulating around me! I had also had this niggling feeling over the past couple of weeks that I needed to be aiming higher in my manifestations, so this was a damn clear universal sign, once again.

With this newfound writer's boost and the motivation I needed, I snuck out of my shift early from my part-time job, as I felt this huge urgency to get home and start writing! It was like a huge wave of excitement and motivation rushing through my body. I even walked into my house dancing. Anyway, I'm not worried about the repercussions of walking out of my shift that was meant to finish at 4 pm. I have arrived home. It's currently 12 pm, in case you were wondering how early my inspired ass left work. I ate some leftover pizza from last night, had a lovely coffee and had a shower to wash away the energy from this morning's interactions. I have fully prepared myself to sit down and allow the words to fall out of me. I have lit candles all around, covered my laptop and desk in crystals and chucked on my comfy clothes. I am here for this. This is me fully trusting the universe; this is me harnessing this important cosmic time.

I told myself that tonight I would write out my ideal life to invite it in whilst this portal is at its peak. However, sitting here now, I'm thinking ... this ideal life that I have been picturing and manifesting over the past couple weeks ... I'm not really aiming quite as high as I should be. I'll give you a little rundown. Okay, so, recently I have been manifesting more people to join my Raise Your Vibe program so I can set up my Jeep Wrangler (which I manifested by the way) with a rooftop tent, a new surfboard and fridge. Then I can drive around Australia, living out of my car, catching some sun and waves, whilst doing card readings and running my programs on the road to make money. I'm actually laughing at myself right now as I read over that because yesterday, I thought this goal was aiming high. Today, after tapping into this lion's gate portal energy, I can feel my dream home being built into my future. I can see myself travelling the world, catching sun, waves and a mint tan (hopefully not Covid-19, lol)! I can see myself holding events to heal and connect with others. I can feel the abundance of being able to financially support myself and my family so we can live our best lives. This new vision will be my life. Just wait.

The whole point of this chapter, really, is so I have a record of what my crazy ass gets up to and the shift I've made whilst connecting to this lion's gate cosmic energy. I've also decided that over the next four days, whilst this energy is still around, I'm going to harness its full potential and smash out this damn book. I'm inviting in my future.

***

P.S. It's 2:22 pm.

16

Cracking Me Open

My boyfriend and I stayed together for four and a half years, and, honestly, even though there were some undesirable times and lessons that I needed to learn from this relationship, we had some of the best times of my life and we got along so well the majority of the time. I am so grateful for him being a part of this life with me. I feel like we had a soul-mate relationship, and I will always have so much love for him. I also feel like this was a karmic relationship, put on my path to test me and awaken me to who I truly am.

Naturally, our four-and-a-half-year relationship came to an end after an argument at the local pub – what a classic young-love ending. The little argument was more him cracking it at me because I wanted to go home early but I didn't want to go back to his house alone. I guess I could have grown the balls to go home alone, but I, being difficult – oh, well, can't change the past. Once home, I wasn't at all happy and slightly embarrassed about the way I was spoken to in front of my friends and the random people that surrounded us at the pub, and I feel the few drinks I had that night gave me the courage to mumble the 'I don't think we should be together anymore' line. To my surprise, he agreed in anger. Then, in his true fashion, turned the light off, rolled over and went to sleep. How can some people just fall asleep like that? On that note, I've got no bloody idea … someone please tell me?

I didn't get a wink of sleep that night, thinking over and over, *I can't believe it's actually over*. I guess I should have been somewhat prepared. It wasn't a complete out-of-the-blue shock, as I had been receiving the 'time to go' card in almost every love reading I had done on myself for the past four months, and I had mentioned to my girlfriend earlier that night that I thought I wanted to leave him. Plus, I always had that inner niggling feeling that we weren't right together, but I always dismissed this as my own insecurities and self-doubt, talking myself into staying in this relationship, telling myself to stop thinking negative.

I ended up leaving his house at 5 am after tossing and turning for hours. I felt the alcohol would have left my system by this time so I was safe to drive, plus I had work the next day and wanted to get home for some sleep before my shift. I drove home crying and started coming to terms with the fact that the relationship had ended. I kept thinking back to all the good times – my mind was uncontrollable. Once home, I cried myself to sleep. I felt like my heart was in a million pieces; my chest was in actual physical pain. I got a solid two and a half hours sleep before I was up for work. As I was getting ready for work, I was trying to concentrate on just getting through the day, trying to pull myself together, telling myself not to think about the break-up until the day was over. I wondered if he was awake yet. I wondered if he was hurting as bad as I was. I ended up sending him a text. It was something along the lines of: *Thank you for an amazing four and a half years. I appreciate everything you have done for me.* I feel this message was my way of confirming that it was definitely over. A few hours later, I got a similar response, him thanking me for the good times we had shared. This is when I knew it was 100% done. I lasted a solid four hours at work before I couldn't do it anymore and went home 'sick' – is heartbreak a sickness? I sure had convinced myself I was terminally ill and dying, thinking my life had come to an end. I called my best pal, Jacqui, on my drive home from work, bawling my eyes out, telling her about everything as she was at the pub with us the night before. The girls met me at my place and dragged me out to Ash's aunty's house, where she was house-sitting. The last thing I wanted to do was leave my home but I knew I needed to be with my girls and keep myself busy. They were the best support I could have ever imagined. I spent the next two nights on Ash's aunty's couch, surrounded by my snotty tissues, an endless supply of chocolate, alcohol and the fluffy socks the girls had bought me. I love fluffy socks – they are my fave thing ever. Even though I was a mess, I felt so supported and loved. I am so grateful for my girls.

I knew I had to get off the couch and come back to reality. The next week was the hardest. I cried so fucking much. I cried in the shower, to my dad, to my sister, to my sister's boyfriend, in the car every time I was alone. I called Jacqui or Ash at least once a day for a sooking session. All I could think about was what I had lost. I lost my lifestyle. I lost my identity. I thought I would lose so many friends, and I did, not because of the break-up, though, but because of the changes I had within myself. I was missing our dog, Kodah, we shared, and I still miss him so much I could cry. I am lucky I still have my little Phineus. I kept thinking of the good times but I needed to keep reminding myself of how unhappy I was with this person. I had to keep reminding myself that I knew it didn't feel right, and that I didn't want that type of relationship anymore. I want a relationship with someone who wants to build a future with me, and this was something he couldn't wrap his head around. I want to build a future with someone where I have no doubt, I feel heard and there's unconditional love for one another. I want the fiery consuming soul-mate love that most of us crave.

Months on, I was still dealing with the break-up, dealing with seeing a new guy, and with my ex coming back into the picture, trying to get me back. I was so overwhelmed and was trying to navigate my way through it all, trying to figure out what was 'meant to be'. I didn't see this new guy for very long, as it was all too much for me, but he played a vital purpose on my journey. He opened my eyes to the kind of energy I wanted to be around. Even though our time together was brief, he impacted my life in the most incredible way. I will always be grateful, and I will always have love for him.

My ex spent a few months trying very hard to get me back, telling me everything I had always wanted to hear, trying to manipulate and guilt me back into a relationship with him. He told me he no longer wanted to live and was making suicidal comments, triggering my guilt further. I couldn't believe I had made someone feel like they wanted to die. It made me sick and I just wanted to make him happy again, even if it meant sacrificing my own happiness in the process. I couldn't work out why I wasn't over the moon with the fact that he finally wanted the life I had always dreamed of with him – something just felt off. Maybe it was the manipulation, or the guilt I felt for knowing deep down that I was going to hurt him for not wanting this life anymore. I felt so selfish for wanting to prioritise myself during the time we spent apart that I just couldn't take it anymore. I wanted to make him happy again.

Whilst I was struggling with what's 'meant to be' and whether or not getting back with my ex was the right decision, the universe decided to throw another fucking laff at me. This sucked, but now I'm laughing because I knew all along what path I was meant to take. I just decided to take the comfortable, familiar, seemingly predictable option, instead of trusting my intuition and inner knowing. I finally decided and told myself that trying again with him was the right thing to do. The decision to date him again created a battle within for far too long. Indecisiveness left me overwhelmed and overthinking. It made trusting my intuition even harder as I kept letting all this pressure I placed around myself build up, causing anxiety, and when I'm anxious, I cannot make sense of the simplest of situations, let alone make a decision about what I think is going to be the rest of my life. Particularly when in crisis, it is impossible to listen to my inner guidance – fear takes over.

I can't even begin to explain how lost I was at this point. I felt for some reason that I needed to be with him, even though I didn't want to, but then I felt guilty for not wanting to? But then I did want to? And then I didn't want to again? I was up and down like crazy. I kept telling him I needed to be alone so I could go down my spiritual path, but he didn't understand, getting angry and expecting me to go down my spiritual path whilst with him. I wished I had the strength to lift both of us onto this spiritual path, but you cannot force someone down a path they are not prepared to walk.

I was a mess and couldn't make sense of anything. I wanted so badly to be able to trust my intuition during this time, but I kept letting my mind get in the way with my chronic overthinking. I told myself that we were 'meant to be'; he just needed a break to 'change and become the best partner a girl could have'; I thought he wanted to 'give me the world and treat me like a queen'; and, I also told myself that he must 'love me so much' now. I knew deep down that this wasn't right for me – you know, that inner knowing coming up again – but I had painted this picture in my head of getting back together and living happily ever after, and this time around, he was painting the picture too! This time around, he had taken over the painting, making it bigger, brighter and oh so much better! This was all too good to be true. I ignored my intuition, my gut feelings and my heart, so the universe had to whack me back into line. Far out, this was a whack and a half. About a month after we had started seeing each other again, my ego thought it was going well. He was planning incredible dates and we were going on amazing adventures, but my body felt off. I should have listened to my intuition. In hindsight, though, if I had listened to my intuition prior to this, I would have never learned how powerfully intuitive I am and how powerful my inner knowing is. Get ready for this. One night, as we were getting ready to go out and see some live music together, which would have been another amazing date, he tells me he's sleeping with someone else! *Sleeping with someone else???* And it had been going on most of the time he was chasing me and convincing me that I was all he ever wanted. *After spending months trying to get me back, he's sleeping with someone else?? Hahaha.* For fuck's sake, universe, this was a good one. Once again, my heart shattered into one million pieces. This was honestly the last thing I ever expected from him. This is what I get for not listening to that inner knowing! I told you my life was seriously a joke during this time.

I continued seeing him anyway because I was so beaten down, and he promised he wouldn't see her again, but he did. So then I finally called it quits, for the last time. I felt a huge weight had lifted off me. I felt like I was finally where I was meant to be. I no longer felt the guilt for wanting to be alone. I felt more in alignment than ever before. I always felt this relationship was out of alignment for me, but I never knew that the feeling was one of being out of alignment. I remember at a couple of points in time when we tried to get back together that even my body rejected him. I would get a UTI (urinary tract infection) before I would see him or we had a date planned – *Every. Single. Time.* – which ensured no impulse of sexual connection, no rush of chemicals to the brain making me think I was in love all over again. My body was telling me to stay away. I learnt to listen to my body from this experience. My body knows what's best for me more than my mind does; it acts in incredible ways. Oh, and guess what? I haven't had a UTI or even the slightest hint of one since leaving him for the last time; isn't that insane?!

After it ended, I couldn't help but be so mad at myself. I thought I had become this badass spiritual bitch who could feel the feels, you know? I started to doubt my abilities to read people and my intuition, but then I woke up to the bullshit self-doubt I was once again feeding myself. My gut and heart were telling me it wasn't right. I didn't need to have the thought that he was playing up behind my back – my gut and heart feeling off should have been enough for me to not go back. My intuition was spot on. I just didn't listen.

I wasn't aware that one of the main reasons I was feeling so lost whilst in my relationship for so long was because I was going through a spiritual awakening. This relationship ending cracked me open. All the pain I was feeling caused all my past pain that I had buried to resurface and rush into my space of awareness. I felt the pain of rolling the car. I felt the miscarriage all over again. I felt childhood trauma rising. I felt my fear of not being loved. It was all overwhelming me. I was cracked the fuck open. I could not bury these emotions and trauma that had been entrenched within my subconscious any longer. Going through this break-up was way harder than I thought it would be. Maybe this was because I wasn't just going through a break-up; I was also going through a damn spiritual awakening. Nevertheless, the number one thing that helped me survive my break-up (and I say *survive* because I had convinced myself that I could die from heartbreak, *haha*) was the story I told myself. I told myself that I needed this ending to step into the real me – 'find myself', to put it in classic young-chick terms. And guess what? That's exactly what happened, because I believed it! But for me, it was so much more than finding myself. It was stepping into my purpose, my higher self, my soul mission and finally becoming aware of the fact that I was going through a spiritual awakening. I will always honour myself now. It is not selfish to make myself the most important person in my life. Being alone is where I found my power. Leaving my relationship forced me to turn inward for my journey of self-realisation.

'Heart is in recovery mode, getting to know itself again. It's as though it wasn't yours for a long time. It wasn't being honoured. Now it feels at peace, at home.' – Rebecca, my incredible reiki practitioner.

***

I now bless this ending, for it cracked me open into my new beginning.

17

Lost and Getting to Know Myself

When the relationship ended, I was learning who I was. I no longer had a relationship to fit my internal or external identity. Who was I?

I can't even describe how lost I felt. I was lost career-wise, friendship-wise and within myself, and I had no idea why I felt like this. I have said *lost* so many times now. Surely by now you know I was lost? I just want to make it clear. I was SO DAMN LOST. I cannot believe I shaped my entire self around this relationship. I had now lost my identity. I found myself getting to know me on a deeper level, as I wasn't occupied, consumed or defined by a partner anymore. The best way I can describe this is like learning a second language as I started to face my buried true self. At the start, I had a slight idea of what I was communicating to the outside world and my internal world. Then things became a little clearer. I started to understand parts of me here and there. Things that resonated with who I truly am started to appear. I gained a better understanding of what actually lights ME up. Then, eventually, after some time, I found this second language was becoming rather familiar and comfortable to speak. I was learning new things about myself every day. It was like I was dating myself. I once feared doing things alone, but now I took myself on beach dates, coffee dates and even lunch dates. I learnt how to love my own company, even in public.

I was making a profound shift in identity.

I went through the classic party phase on my way to discovering myself, catching up with all my friends that I had lost contact with during my relationship. I was living it up with my newfound freedom, chasing temporary happiness. Once single, the occasional party drug usage became more frequent and I kept telling myself, *You're just having some single life fun.* Then I found myself wanting to 'get off my face' more often. It was like an unconscious longing of wanting to escape myself – because on nights out, I was temporarily free from my mind. I would take myself to a state that was below thinking – well, this is the best way to describe it. Instead of raising my state and separating myself from thought, I removed thought all together with the use of substance. I was in two minds about it, though, knowing that I didn't really need to be doing it and the split side of 'I want to have the utmost fun', 'live my best life', and the classic 'everyone else is doing it'. I feel I easily could have continued down this path for longer. However, my awakening was calling me and I knew I needed to rise above and snap the fuck out of this party phase. It began to feel more and more wrong. After pushing myself to my limits a few times, the guilt for the next week was unbearable, not to mention the comedown. I knew that I should probably look at putting a stop to the drugs. I knew it was hindering my growth and I shouldn't be using them to block out the intense anxiety that came hand in hand with my awakening, but I didn't know there was a reason for my super sensitivity at this stage. My body had become so sensitive to everything, including certain foods, so drugs were the worst thing for me, but my ego mind kept making excuses, as I found my ego mind always wanted me to stay in a state of suffering. *It's okay. You're just having some single-life fun. Everyone goes off the rails for a bit after a break-up.* This was the way my mind was justifying my behaviour and complete lack of responsibility. I was struggling to shake the excuses I was making, which were preventing me from fully stepping into my spiritual self, finding it easier to just escape.

Whilst growing up, I believe I was very in tune with my spiritual side, as most children are, but I feel I lost touch with my gifts as I got older – they were conditioned out of me through my surroundings. Whilst on my journey of figuring out who I was, I realised all this. I needed to let this side of me in to reveal who I was, but why was it so hard? I felt a greater block, fear, and lack of belief and trust within myself around all this 'woo, woo' stuff when I started to enter my teen years. I would play around with cards and some people around me would question it, which, in turn, made me question myself. It always felt like there was something else blocking me from fully stepping into this life – I just couldn't put my finger on it for quite some time. I was terrified of it, terrified of putting my hippie side on show to the world for fear of how others would react to me. I battled with this for years. I have memories of making cubby houses and playing with what my mum calls and what I thought were 'imaginary friends'. However, after doing a few past-life regression sessions over the last few months, I have now realised that these imaginary friends were actually spirits or my spirit guides; spirit guides are spirits that follow us through life, guiding us and protecting us. My mum even bought me a cat when I was four years old, and I named her after one of my 'imaginary friends'. I feel this may have been to distract me from all this 'woo, woo' spiritual stuff. Getting me a black cat – yep, that really did the trick. I felt like a full-blown witch now. My cat, Moga, passed away not long after I had fully embraced my awakening. It's like she knew it was time.

I managed to push past the fear one day at a time, choosing not to shrink myself to protect someone else's ego. After pushing past this fear and fully stepping into my spiritual path, I later uncovered that all my fear was not coming from my current life; it was from a past-life trauma. Spirituality is something that has been majorly oppressed over the centuries. My fear of opening up to this life was coming from past-life and generational trauma. In the past, we were persecuted for having spiritual beliefs, and were branded 'witches' and murdered, just for our spiritual beliefs and gifts. So, for some people in this time, it can be quite hard to open up, as we have this entrenched fear within our being telling us it's not safe. We are living in a time now when it is safe to wake up. It is safe to tune in to our gifts. It is more widely accepted now. Now is a time for the great awakening. Many people are waking up at this time because it is safe to. The collective view is being shifted.

When I decided I wanted to fully open myself to this witchy life, I was flooded with signs. I started noticing repetitive numbers EVERYWHERE! I started hearing repetitive songs. I'd see the same cars with the same numbers on them every day. So much synchronicity. Synchronicity means simultaneous occurrences of events that appear significantly related but have no discernible causal connection. I started getting the niggling feeling that these were signs, as I have always been a big believer in 'everything happens for a reason' and nothing is a coincidence. I started to look up these numbers, trying to figure out why I was seeing them. A common one at the start was 444, a number meaning your angels and spirit guides are with you. Others were 11:11, 12:12 and 888. The common theme around these numbers that kept coming up was 'spiritual awakening'. I didn't really pay it much mind as I didn't understand what it meant. I thought maybe it was just saying that I was becoming more spiritual and more open to receiving signs or something.

The numbers kept appearing. I couldn't ignore them – they were always under my nose. They were coming at me all hours of the day, so I started to note them down and their meanings. I had the longest list in my notes on my phone of all these numbers I kept seeing. I wanted to learn more; I just didn't know where to start. I learnt that receiving synchronicity is a common part of stepping into your spiritual life – these numbers are here to guide us. These synchronicities can come in any form.

Once I believed in synchronicity and that it was happening at the perfect time for a reason, I started to tune in to these messages and what they meant. These numbers that were getting communicated to me were a reflection of my own inner guidance, showing me what had been niggling at me in my internal world out in my external surroundings. It's not a coincidence that you see 555, which means abundance, as you are flicking through job ads. You feel me? Some days, I would start yelling at my spirit guides because I would let my mind overwhelm me. 'What do you mean?' I would scream whilst getting flooded with numbers on my peak-hour drive home. I have now noticed that I tend to get flooded with numbers a few days before I'm about to shift to a whole other level of consciousness and improve my state of being. Right before I shift into a higher state, I'm filled with self-doubt. I feel lower energies and emotions – these are just being processed and released – and the numbers I receive are great confirmation that I am headed to the next level. I put so much pressure on myself about whether I was on the right path or not, causing so much strife, all because of my inability to trust the universe, always wanting to jump to the next thing. I now know I am always on the right path, whether I'm having a lower moment or not, and the amount of peace this belief creates is incredible. Numbers are one of the main ways I receive guidance. I love it. I never feel alone.

During my unaware stages of my awakening, I was consumed by my conscious mind. I was a chronic over-thinker, trying to make sense of everything that was happening to me, constantly feeling drained and overwhelmed. But, of course, I battled with this because my ego mind couldn't make sense of all these signs and intuitive hits I would receive – it just couldn't comprehend soul messages. Overthinking was the biggest cause of unnecessary pain. When I got overwhelmed, I needed to tune in to my body, but I was so caught up within my mind that even when I did tune in to my body, I wasn't listening to what it was telling me. I would try to reason with my ego mind. I would always be asking, 'Why?' I would get so tangled up. I had no control, and let my mind control me. I would get so frustrated with myself for not being able to tune in to my body for that clear guidance I needed, getting flooded with anxiety in my chest, making it impossible to feel anything my intuition was communicating to me. I hated living in my mind, and with meditation, I have learnt to quiet the chatter in my head.

Trusting my intuition was something I struggled with for far too long and I learnt the hard way. As I was getting to know myself, I started turning to my inner guidance system, my intuition, my instinctive knowing not defined by conscious reasoning. I was learning how to tune in to my body and feel from my soul/higher self. I felt it and sensed it guiding me. It was not a process of thought – my intuition gave me the ability to know something without the mind. I found so much discomfort in trusting my intuition because it was something that my mind couldn't comprehend. The more I thought about it, the more confused I got.

I feel my intuition is a bridging between my instinct and reason, unconscious and conscious mind. I find myself getting a gut feeling or a feeling in my chest, or a vision – that is my intuition telling me something. I have started tuning into my body, noticing how it feels in certain situations, when I am about to make a decision. If something doesn't feel quite right within my chest, and I have a tight or heavy feeling, this is intuition telling me that this path will not serve my highest good, purely not aligning with me in this current moment. This isn't to say this path will not align with me in the future, but for now, my intuitive senses are saying that this isn't in alignment. On the flip side of things, if something is in alignment with me, my heart centre feels lighter, flooded with a feeling of love or warmth.

My intuitive senses were often confused or manipulated by my mind as my ego couldn't find reasoning behind it, so I stopped asking the dreaded 'why?' question, trusting my intuitive feelings and the universe. Practice makes for improvement. From time to time, I would go against what my heart and gut were telling me, and the universe would repay me with testing times, as I was choosing the hard path. Also I just want to note, I believe that nothing we experience is good or bad – it is just how we label it. I firmly believe the seemingly 'bad times' are for lessons, growth and positive changes. Shifting into this mindset has allowed me to overcome everything life has tossed my way.

Anyway, back to it. To when my intuition was telling me that I wasn't meant to be with my ex-partner anymore, but I tried again with him anyway, going against my gut and what my heart was telling me. One day, shortly after we decided to try again at our relationship, my heart was physically hurting in his presence. I ignored this, but later found out he was sleeping with someone else whilst seeing me. That was a wake-up call and a half. I needed that kick up the ass to listen and trust intuition. I had many opportunities where I could have learnt this lesson in an easier, less harsh way, but I wasn't consciously mindful of lessons within situations and trusting my gut. I needed something extreme like heartbreak and a blow to the ego to teach me a lesson. Feeling my way around my intuition and learning to trust it was a vital part of my awakening journey. I recognised the incredible guidance system that we all carry within ourselves. I stopped looking for answers in my external world and turned inward. Now I feel my way through. I centre myself, calm myself, and feel. And now that I trust my intuition, I no longer feel like I am making decisions alone. The bond with my higher self is the most important relationship I will ever have.

My inner guidance system often seems to disregard the otherwise seemingly convincing reality of the outer world.

As I started to tune in to my intuition and my body, I noticed how highly sensitive I was to others. During my childhood, I was spiritually sensitive and drained. My mother had convinced me and those around me that I had an actual medical condition because of my tiredness (maybe it was just you fuckers draining me, *haha*). They put it down to low iron, but there was no way I had low iron 24/7. I ate well and I was forced to eat meat, which was something that I strongly disliked. I remember trying not to throw up night after night as I was force-fed the red meat that so deeply did not resonate with who I was and who I am at a soul level. Being in a family of men that went 'hunting' meant that it was never the death of the animal that made me hate eating meat, even though my family would constantly question me with that look of judgement as if I was the odd one for not enjoying this. *Pffffft*. It even felt like sometimes they were trying to make me believe that I didn't enjoy meat because of hurting animals. It seems like this was a way they could understand me. I often felt misunderstood. I purely did not like the taste and the way meat made me feel. It just seemed extremely unnatural to me. Then I discovered what an empath was. An empath will absorb others' emotional and energy states as if they are their own, and commonly even the physical pains of others, often leaving these beings overwhelmed and drained of energy. Imagine carrying around another person's energy and being completely unaware. Imagine never knowing how to release all this rubbish. I was an unaware empath, walking around depleting my energy in almost every interaction I faced. Social situations, working in a crowded office, mindlessly scrolling social media – these things were unknowingly sucking the life out of me.

Now that I had a reason behind my lifetime of being tired and drained, I needed to learn how to protect my energy. I began to tune in to my body, asking myself if I was holding the emotions or energy of others within my energy field. I started to notice if I felt a certain way for no apparent reason in day to day life – this was a sign that I had picked up on someone else's energy. I tuned into my body through meditation and just became more consciously aware.

I am now able to instantly and easily recognise when I am carrying weight that isn't mine. The key to being an empowered empath, for me, is by being so familiar with my energy and my body that I can sense straight away when I have picked up something that isn't mine. At these times, I notice a sudden depleting of my vibe and a draining of my energy.

To protect my energy, I use healing crystals, such as black tourmaline, to absorb any energy that doesn't serve me. I also imagine myself surrounded in white light, shielding me from others' energy. I have also learnt how to cut energy cords with people, and I cannot explain the release I feel when I do this. I need to be mindful that I'm not using this gift and my ability to pick up on feelings and emotions as a way to infringe on someone's boundaries. I have done this in the past – only with good intentions, of course – but sometimes people truly do want to be left alone. This is another key to keeping my energy high.

The day I realised I was an empath was the day I felt like I truly understood why I am so overly sensitive and easily drained. It wasn't low iron, after all. I am an alone-time loving, highly intuitive, empathetic empath. I was like a super excited kid in a toy store! What else can I discover about myself?! What other beliefs have been drummed into me? I had to be impacted too harshly by others' energy to realise how powerful energy is.

Protect your energy. Because I am so sensitive to energy, I needed to ensure I protected it.

Cutting cords is a common spiritual practice that ensures energy recovery, removing energy ties from people and situations that no longer serve our highest good. When we connect to people through conversation and interactions, we create energy ties with them, a stream of energy causing us to interact on a much deeper level and creating the ability to tune in to each other's energy, consciously or unconsciously. If we do not cut cords, we are keeping that energy stream open, not allowing ourselves to fully release the past or people, and not creating space for the new. Keeping energy cords open depleted my energy astronomically.

I wanted to pop this little story in this book as I believe it was a super powerful moment for me. Once I was officially done and dusted with my relationship, I knew it was time to cut energy cords with my ex-partner. As I moved through life, growing, changing and evolving, I found it necessary to let go of that which no longer served me. When we let go, we create space for the new.

The day I cut cords with my ex was super intense. I set my room up, lit candles, burnt sage, really creating a comforting space. I made it like a full ceremony for me, allowing this to be my celebration of releasing the past. I lay on my bed, the smell of candles and sage filling my lungs. I tuned into my breath, allowing myself to centre before I started my visualisation. Once centred and calm, with my eyes closed, I visualised my ex standing in front of me – we were bonded with a glowing gold cord of energy from our stomachs. I looked over to the left of me and I saw archangel Michael standing there with his giant sword, ready to cut our energy ties. I gave him permission to cut the cord. He raised his sword, and *slice*, the gold cord was cut! The glimmering gold slowly faded away, as did the image of my ex standing in front of me. I felt different, and a sense of release, but I can't quite explain it. Then, I felt this heart-wrenching feeling come over me. It was like I had lost him all over again. I was doing that thing where I cry and cannot breathe – classic me. I couldn't get the air in. It was painful, like a silent cry, as the tears streamed down my face. I allowed myself to feel this extreme grief, and at the time, I didn't realise I was purging; the hysterical tears were the release of energy. I was free. I try to cut cords frequently these days, as I get so exhausted from daily interactions. It isn't nearly as traumatic as that experience I just described. I just ask my angels some days to cut cords with any interactions I've had from the day or the past week – cutting ties and creating the space I need because of my sensitivity to energy.

My self-confidence and self-doubt ruled me, crippling me and holding me hostage. I identified with this doubt. It was me. It was who I was. Prior to waking up, I wasn't even aware that there was something holding me back, or that this was something that I could overcome. Some days, I would feel as though I was being physically choked by my thoughts and feelings. Relating to my hesitation to do things, I would talk myself out of everything. I had zero motivation and zero confidence that anything I did would actually bring me some sense of joy, so I didn't try. It was also during this time that I realised I am more attuned to giving back to others, as receiving was uncomfortable for me. Even the smallest of things, like having the urge to paint something or draw – outlets I enjoyed in the past – instantly I would talk myself out of. I didn't even consider that doing these things could light me up, and I didn't care. I was stubbornly stuck in the continuous loop of lower emotions, with no faith in a way out.

Now, doubt is different to fear. Fear definitely holds us back and can be crippling. However, at this time, I hadn't even allowed myself to get to the fear stage as I just purely believed I couldn't do anything I wanted to do. I couldn't even wrap my head around the fact that I deserved anything good in this world or that I deserved happiness, which sounds absolutely ridiculous now. Every single person on this earth can choose to live their damn best life. We just need to have the confidence in ourselves and the universe to pursue it. Now thinking back to this time, I'm still unsure where this crippling lack of confidence in myself came from or when it exactly started! I'm feeling like it was maybe a build-up of a heap of little things causing me to doubt who I was. I'd always dream big, but never really took enough action, as I thought I would never reach anything that great. I never fully pursued something from my heart either, as I would always find a way to talk myself out of it. I knew I had to get past this. I knew this would hinder my future if I didn't. Far out, it was hard to take this step because I didn't have the faith that it was something I could get past. I couldn't see the way out. I needed to shift the entire state of how I perceived myself.

I set out to break down this wall of self-doubt! It was a long process as this was something that was instilled deep into my subconscious, but I was up for the challenge with the support of my mentor. I also just want to note – reaching out for support doesn't make you 'weak', as the old me believed. Reaching out for support gave me that extra strength I needed to push through this challenging period of astounding growth. When I wanted to give up, or didn't believe I could do it anymore, my mentor was there, filling me with the little bit of extra belief I couldn't pull from my own self yet. Ways of breaking down this wall included journaling to get to the root of why I didn't believe in myself and my abilities, but I didn't find this that impactful as I couldn't find a root cause. However, the one task that had a huge impact was every morning when I woke up, I would visualise myself kicking down a large, red, brick wall that represented my self-doubt. Some days, I would kick through the wall; others, I wouldn't even make an indent no matter how hard I tried. But I kept at it, committed to change and committed to what lived beyond this wall. One day, I smashed through this wall, sending the entire weight of the red bricks crashing down to the ground with a loud thud, and I climbed over the crumbled bricks. Once on the other side of this wall, I felt a huge shifting occur within. I felt powerful. I felt like I could do anything at all in this world. The large part of my self-doubt was gone! This was a pivotal moment along my journey. I later discovered that this self-doubt and striving for perfection has travelled through four generations, and that it's not actually me speaking to myself in this way. It's not me who questions my every move. It has been passed onto me from my ancestors. Once aware of this, I could separate this self-doubt and negative self-talk from myself, as it is not me, just like I did with my ego.

This is the power of the mind in action.

Once I broke through the doubt I previously drowned in, I found myself inviting in and visualising my dream life. I also made the effort to visualise my higher self/ideal self every morning in front of me, and then step into that being and become what it is that I envision my future self as. I'd ask myself, *What is my heart calling for?* Without this high wall of doubt blocking me, I could see into my heart with much more clarity. *What do I want out of life? What lights me up?* This is when I felt excited about life for the first time! In the past, I would get excited about things that were coming up in life, like getting a new car or finishing a course, for example – these things were external to me but contributed to how I defined myself. And at this stage, I was still deep within my ego, as you have probably realised. Until crossing this hurdle and shifting out of ego, I had never actually been excited to be alive. I had never been excited for all the possibility that awaits me, and the future I could dream into reality. Don't get me wrong – it's not like I hid in a hole of sadness, never getting excited for things, because I did! I'd get so excited, but as I said before, it was just for things external to me. I believed I could create anything I wanted in life now. The next step in this journey was pushing past the fear of acting on my heart's desires, which I will get to.

I had taken some huge steps on my journey of getting to know myself, tuning into my intuition, discovering I am a highly sensitive empath, and pushing past my deeply instilled self-doubt, but I still had no idea I was in the midst of a spiritual awakening. I still felt lost and confused and continued to think something was wrong with me, like I was going mad.

***

I am finally getting to know my soul.

Little Life Update

The past week, I have been letting my ego and self-doubt creep back in. I have been struggling with consistency, keeping going, and committing to this book. Writing does take up so much time, and my ego is telling me that I should be working on things that actually provide an income. I have been doubting whether this book will help people, or whether people even want to hear my story. But you know what? If hearing my story helps just one person, I will be over the moon. I know deep down I need to write this book and share it with the world; ego has just cast a brief shadow over my light. I will shine brighter. I have lived many lifetimes to get me to this one. I know what is flowing on into these pages is channelling through me from past lives, spirit guides and other beings. I'm being called to share this. Yes, my human body is young, but my soul is eternal and has lived many lifetimes.

This book is a powerful shadow work in play. Writing is my healing, my passion, my strength. Shadow work is facing the darker thought processes that our human ego holds. During my awakening is when I became aware of these processes. Exploration of my shadow self and darker aspects of my being allows me to further connect with my soul.

18

Phases of Awakening

These next chapters are the phases of my spiritual awakening I experienced and how I navigated my way through all these life-altering shifts that were occurring, shifting my perspective and life.

I just want to touch on how I want to keep this book as 'real-life' as possible. I'm sitting here trying to map out these chapters and the perfect order in which I want to explain my spiritual awakening journey. I just have to spit these words out and explain how I'm currently feeling. I feel so overwhelmed. I am so passionate about these experiences that I want them to come across in the best way and order possible. Now as I write, I'm thinking, the order does not matter, because all these situations and phases came and went, then reappeared, then disappeared again, then grew, then altered, so on and so forth. So, I guess, what I'm trying to say is, don't pay much mind to the order of these chapters, as some things overlapped, lingered around or only lasted a short while. I'm feeling much lighter now, like the pressure that was coming from my mind has been lifted as I answered the call and the niggle to write down my current feelings. It's insane how easily things channel through you when you move over and allow them to.

19

My Spiritual Awakening Discovery

Finally, I was no longer putting up resistance and refusing to wake up, and, instead, was listening to my body and soul. After my four-and-a-half-year relationship ended, I felt such heightened anxiety and struggled to cope with all the energy around me. I was hypersensitive, and this was all a huge part of my awakening, becoming super sensitive to everything around me, way more than ever before. Every day was a struggle to get out of bed as I would wake up thinking about my ex-partner and all that I had lost and how much my life had changed. My mind was my worst enemy at this point in time. I hated going to work because I would always leave feeling so flat, like the life had been sucked out of me. This hit me so hard during one period I stayed in my room for a solid week straight, only leaving for food and water to survive. *Yeesssss, I know* – I was feeling super sorry for myself, but I didn't know how else to make myself feel better. I just couldn't handle any form of interaction. I was the skinniest I had ever been and hated looking in the mirror at my pin legs, and boxy, lanky shape. I think it was the stress I was putting on myself that made me drop some weight, not the lack of eating. I just couldn't get my mind to stop.

I thought my added anxiety and depression was all due to the break-up, but I slowly started to realise over the next couple of months, as my emotions towards my ex dwindled away in intensity, that the anxiety and depression were still there. Even though I was starting to feel better each day, and had stopped feeling so sorry for myself, I also began convincing myself that I wasn't going to be forever alone, which sounds so ridiculous now as I enjoy being single at this stage in my life. I was taking note of the fact that I didn't have any reason to be feeling like this; well, no reason that was great enough to justify the intense levels of anxiety I was feeling. So why was I feeling like this? This is when I was starting to question everything a little more deeply. I was putting the work in to keep a positive mindset, so why wasn't this crippling anxiety disappearing? I found once I arrived at work, I was riddled with anxiety again.

During this time, I was working in an office with around forty other people in close proximity to me at any given time. The people in this office, in my opinion, were over-worked, stressed and sleeping their way through life. I was feeling and taking on all their energy! There were so many energies and emotions hitting me as I walked into the office each day, which immediately felt like anxiety rushing through my body. This was all a part of my awakening; my entire state of being was extremely sensitive to others' energy; it was unlike anything I had ever experienced before. Due to my intense sensitivity, I retreated to the comfort of my home, only leaving if I absolutely had to. I found myself questioning absolutely everything in my life, my beliefs, my judgements, my conditioning, and the way I lived my life, especially the more I got familiar with my intuition. I hid away in a cocoon of self-realisation, questioning society, everything that shaped me, and the way I flowed through life – actually, more like the way I didn't flow through life. The more I questioned everything, the more I expanded my awareness.

This was a whole new level of homebody for me. I wasn't entirely sure why this was happening, and, little did I know, this was all an essential phase of my awakening, drawing me closer to my discovery. I like to call this the 'hermit phase'. Whilst in my cocoon of discovering myself, locking myself away in my room as often as I could, I started watching hundreds and hundreds of YouTube videos, and this is when I discovered what a spiritual awakening was! I watched one video explaining a spiritual awakening and the common signs of this epic shift in consciousness, and everything I was feeling started making so much sense – I was onto something here! More videos were popping up on my YouTube. I started to follow people online who spoke about a spiritual awakening. I had never heard this term before this phase of my life so I was instantly intrigued. Then I woke the fuck up to the fact that I was going through a spiritual awakening. A SPIRITUAL EFFING AWAKENING! IT ALL FINALLY MADE SENSE! I had finally figured out what the fuck was wrong with me! I had woken to my soul! It all made sense! I wasn't crazy! I was no longer lost! I was so drawn to this spiritual life for a reason! Once I became aware of my own spiritual awakening, I felt whole for the first time in my life. I felt like the pure consciousness I am. I woke up out of my self-inflicted state of pain and suffering. It was around this time that I separated myself from my mind. This was the greatest freedom from incessant thought. The feeling was indescribable!

I was hooked on all this esoteric stuff! I was up all hours of the night; the internet was my best friend, and self-education was my entire life. I felt like I was finally discovering the answers to all my questions. I no longer felt lost and confused. The more videos I watched, the more books I read, the more I understood all these thoughts, feelings and signs I had been receiving. I learnt all that I could about this phenomenal, seemingly esoteric concept. I couldn't stop myself – every spare moment I had at home and at work, I would chuck my headphones on. When in the car, I would have videos or podcasts playing, finding comfort and release in the understanding I was gaining, and the educational content I had found that perfectly explained my internal world.

This was the period I learnt so much, not only about awakening, but also about the psychology of the human mind, the soul, our higher selves, intuition, psychic abilities, etc., but most of all, who I was. I wanted to stay in this little comfortable learning bubble forever, as it was so incredibly powerful to me, but I knew I needed to venture out into the world. I needed to come out of my cocoon, as much as I didn't want to, and transform into a butterfly.

Now that I was aware that I was, in fact, awake and had started along my healing journey, I struggled to embrace life, and I struggled to be present in the moment, as I was just having so many realisations and thoughts racing through my mind about this incredible life I had stepped into. I kept wanting to retreat back home to journal, think and create some space around myself for some clarity around everything I was channelling through from my higher self. Even at this point in time, I am still learning how to embrace life, be present and allow myself the time for my healing work – it's all about balance. Coronavirus has come at the perfect time for me. I am loving this time for healing and growth. I am so proud of myself for embracing this pandemic and using it in the best possible way for me. Doing the inner work can be hard, confusing, frustrating and overwhelming, but it is by far the best path I have ever decided to venture down. My life changed when I decided to take action and implement the things I had learnt into my daily life. Finally, I was aware of the profound shift I had been embarking on and I was committed to raising my vibe!

If you're feeling trapped within your mind, a slave to your thoughts, I hope reading this frees you. This is the most valuable part of my awakening! I know – big call! So, listen up, make sure you understand this concept. This changed my damn life and it's going to change yours too! This is when I shifted out of my ego and into my awakened glory. Once I understood this, and how to observe the mind, completely disconnect from it, and not identify with it, my anxiety, depression and self-doubt diminished astronomically, as that was all coming from what my ego mind was conjuring up. It was an instant shift for me –

this hit my soul. I am not my mind. So powerful. My mind would wander uncontrollably, running a loop of past experiences and plotting future events, causing anxiety, stress, guilt, fear and more. I was living in the lower vibrational contracted state, being controlled by my egoic mind. I was learning how to notice thought. Just because I had a thought, that didn't mean it was true! It didn't mean the thought was me. I didn't have to choose to become that thought and let it manipulate my days. The greatest lesson I learnt along my journey of raising my vibe and shifting my consciousness into awakening was observing my thoughts. I learnt how to observe my thoughts without labelling them as good or bad – just watch them, realise they are there and then tune back into the present moment. The more I did this, the quieter my thoughts became, and this one was a fucking gift – overthinking would cripple me in the past, leaving me feeling unbearably anxious. I was finally free from my mind.

My mind couldn't comprehend that it didn't need to know every minor detail of what is going to happen next in life. Imagine it like this. When we are driving in the dark, we can only see the next piece of road that the light shines upon. We trust the road is going to continue no matter what, and guess what? It always does. The ego mind doesn't need to know exactly what is coming up ahead (as much as we want to know what's happening next in our lives), just as we don't need to see the next hundred kilometres light up in front of us. We trust. I needed to trust in my soul and intuition, and that everything is mapped out for me, even if I have no idea what it looks like just yet. When I fought my mind, trying to make my thoughts stop racing, I was feeding it more energy. The more I observe the mind and no longer identify with it, the quieter the chatter becomes. Shifting out of my mind made my identity feel freer than ever before, like the weight of society's expectations that I had absorbed dwindled away. What a life-altering rising of consciousness. I felt like I had figured out some huge secret to living a happy life! I was stoked!

It was when I learnt that not only my mind but my entire reality changed. I had finally stepped into a soul-led life.

The early days of my awakening was an odd time. I felt like I had learnt so much – about myself, about the universe – but I had no idea how to present it to the world. I felt a huge urge to show the world this huge internal shift I'd had! And what better way to do it than to dye my hair! Most girls after going through a break-up want to make themselves feel good and show the world that they 'look good, feel good'! It was much the same with me. However, it was more about my internal shift. Reflecting out, I needed to feel like I had changed on the outside too. I went from medium-brown hair to a beautiful light brown-blonde. I was blonde through the majority of high school, and oddly enough, I felt more myself than I had in a long time. I gave dyeing my hair this huge importance, and leading up to dyeing my hair, I told myself that once I had dyed it, it would give me the confidence and power to show the real me to the world. Because I truly believed this, this is exactly what happened – that belief created my reality! The mind is a powerful thing! I put such high value around this change in appearance, and I so deeply believed it would reflect the new me, that it did. I shifted my entire state. I felt a new level of freedom from others' perceptions because I was truly happy and content within myself, for the first time. It is wild how easy it is to love myself when I no longer place value in the way others perceive me.

I have found one of the greatest tools for stepping into the new and becoming the person I want to be is through visualisation every day. This has helped me tremendously. Every single morning, I visualise my ideal self and become it. This is such an easy way I shift my internal identity in order to reflect my ideal self into my external reality. This all comes back to my beliefs. If we believe we are a shy person and see ourselves as that shy person, we become it and reflect this into our external reality. I have the power to see myself as a confident, accomplished, powerful, goddess, or whatever it is I want to be each week! I create my own identity! I visualise my ideal self, the version of me who has already achieved her goals, the me who is glowing with happiness, the me who confidently embraces her uniqueness, standing in front of me. I notice how I look. I notice this energy around the ideal me. Then I simply imagine myself stepping into this person. I become one with this person. This ideal version of me is now me. I look down at my body as I am now my ideal self. On days I don't visualise my ideal self and become it, I seriously notice such a difference in my self-confidence, productivity, and vibe – they are diminished. This helps me to step into alignment, but it also makes me feel fucking incredible every day!

My awakening discovery gifted me my best authentic self. It's okay to grow and change so much that no one knows who you are anymore. Your personality is not fixed; it is flexible and evolving.

***

The more care and energy I put into self-realisation, the more light shines onto my path.

Little Life Update

I'm currently living in week three of Melbourne's six-week, stage-four lockdown due to this worldwide pandemic we all know and loathe called coronavirus. We currently aren't allowed to travel more than 5 km from our place of residence, unless you're an essential worker or providing care. I do get to escape the walls of my home for work two days a week. Can someone please explain to me how interior design is essential? Cannot quite wrap my head around that one. A lot of this doesn't make sense to me. The more I look into conspiracy theories and dive into that rabbit hole ... But that's not what this book is about and I could go on for days – *cough*, people are blatantly unaware and so easily controlled, *cough*. Despite my frustration that I cannot legally dip my body into the icy Mornington Peninsula seas in the midst of winter, I can't help but have a deeper sense of knowing that this is happening, at this specific time, to me, for a reason. Far out, listen to me. I make this worldwide pandemic sound like it's all about me, but seriously! I think this book needs to be birthed and this pandemic is what has cleared the way for its creation. All the souls currently in lockdown struggling with their own spiritual awakening could use a book like this! Not to toot my own horn but – *toot, toot, fuckin' toot* – this is going to help so many people on their awakening journey, and I feel an urgency to get it finished.

As much as the control factor from the government is upsetting me and my spirit of daily adventure is tethered, oddly enough, I don't want this lockdown to end just yet. I feel I have so much to learn and ponder on during this time. The thought of mentioning this to my friends and family makes me cringe. If my friends or family read this right now, they would think I have actually lost the plot more than usual. They cannot wait for this lockdown to be over, and neither can I, but there's just something more to it for me than meets the eye. Everything is flowing in perfect timing. My awakening was triggered. I had the time to drown myself in discovering who I am and understanding the way I operate on a deep level. THEN I was guided to write this book, but wasn't sure how I'd find the time. Then BAM! Stage-four lockdown kicks in, giving me the time and space to really get this cracking. I can picture my dad's frustration if I allowed myself to mutter some words along the lines of wanting to stay in lockdown. Well, just at least until this book is done; then I wouldn't need to find excuses for staying home all the time to write.

Actually, my sister is sitting on the couch near me at the moment. Let's test this theory. 'I don't want this lockdown to end just yet,' I say.

Ky just looks at me in shock with fierce judgement and says, 'I do. I fucken hate it. First time around wasn't too bad, but this time, I want to neck myself.'

Hahaha, and there ya go. 'I'm so fucken bored.' Another classic from Ky as she sits here struggling to cure her boredom. So, yeah, just wanted to say that amid everyone hating life, I'm enjoying the time I have to sit down and write this little book that will hopefully help others along their journey. I know I have lived many lifetimes, all to get me to where I am currently, in the time of the 'great awakening', and the more I write, the more I believe that this book is the reason I'm here. I am always on the right path, learning lessons and navigating my way through.

20

Expanding Awareness

I am now awake and becoming aware of everything that has shaped my reality (and all the times I have messed up big time *haha*). I have committed to expanding my awareness and changing my life. My beliefs were creating my reality, and this was a harsh truth to accept. I didn't want to be responsible for my life and the pity parties I threw for myself. I previously believed that everything happened *to* me, not *for* me. I was stuck in a victim mentality, and because I believed this, these lower vibrational experiences kept happening, and I resented that all these things kept happening to me. The more I thought something, the more I believed it. There was no separation between whatever it was I was thinking, and who I actually was; my deep beliefs drove my behaviours. I needed to strip away many limiting beliefs and attachments to reveal my soul. I had so many beliefs relating and connecting me back to my past, which was also in so many ways limiting my future. I was becoming aware of the beliefs and stories I told myself subconsciously, as they were keeping me in a lower state of vibration.

My subconscious mind is the beliefs, stories, urges and memories that are beyond my conscious mind, meaning I was often unaware of what was limiting me until I brought it to the surface. Therefore, when my beliefs get challenged, it is extremely confronting for me. It feels like my identity and sense of self are getting challenged. It feels like way more than a belief – it feels like who I am.

The stories I told myself were commonly picked up from those around me and also based off past experiences. I was consciously unlearning these in order to grow and free myself from my box. It wanted to hold me in a place of fear, keeping me trapped in this limiting belief cycle and a lower vibrational state. One of the most common stories that I told myself and that is taught in society is we must finish year 12, go to university, get a good job, get married, buy a house and then we are successful in life. I believed this as fact and placed my self-worth around a job that looks great on paper. However, did this job really fuel my passion? Did I love going to this job? The answer is no. Where's the passion? The fire? The joy? None there. This grinds my gears that society does this to us. I put so much pressure on myself after finishing school to find a 'good job', I would literally make myself feel sick over it. I felt worthless because I wasn't going to uni, but I kept telling myself, *There's no point in going to uni if you have no idea what to study, Shay.* So glad I told myself that – didn't mean it took the pressure off, though, as I didn't understand that this was a belief I had, or that I could unlearn it.

I also believed that I wouldn't be able to live without my ex-boyfriend and that I needed him, as he would tell me this over the years of our relationship. This made it hard for me to get over our break-up and step into happiness. I struggled to 'live without him' because of this deeply instilled belief within my subconscious. Once I brought this sucker to the surface, it was so much easier for me to heal from our break-up. Of course, I could live without him. All I needed to do was become aware of what it was that my subconscious was telling me. I also realised that I had created an unconscious belief within myself that no one would love me, and loving someone else became one of my greatest fears. I placed a belief around the one time my boyfriend didn't say he loved me back, and just one small moment in time caused me to believe that no one would love me. Even after he eventually started saying he loved me, I still believed he didn't, because I had told myself so many times and I believed I wasn't loved. I believed I was unlovable, so that was my reality, no matter what the external world was saying to me.

I had *soooo* many limiting beliefs that I have been working on since waking up and I recognised them by how I was shaping my life around certain things I told myself. I believed I couldn't offer card readings because I wasn't that kind of person. I believed I had to be grinding and working hard to get far in life. I believed that I couldn't write an e-book or book of any kind because throughout high school I would tell myself I hated English and was terrible at it. I have now unlearned these perceptions by purely becoming aware of them as limiting beliefs and not fact, and now I'm loving writing this. Limiting beliefs could be anything! It is anything you tell yourself that prevents you from doing something. I had many intense realisations around the beliefs I had during the chaotic early phase of my awakening, and I put so much effort into unlearning these beliefs, as I was set on freeing myself.

I had to face the harsh reality that I invited in every ego struggle I faced. I started to question myself. *Do I love me?* Nope. Then how could I expect someone else to love me if I couldn't even love myself? I didn't believe I was worthy of love, so how could I invite it in?

I stopped looking into my future through a lens of past beliefs.

***

I found myself tuning into my behaviours – whether or not I complained a lot, whether I had mostly positive or self-destructive thoughts running through my mind. I was making myself aware of everything I was doing in my life, how I lived and how to raise my state. I became aware to then shift. Once I became aware that I was following in my mother's footsteps, playing victim, blaming the world, trying to make others feel sorry for me, and looking for opportunities to be the victim way too often, just like she did, in the situations in my own life, I knew it needed to stop. It felt good in the moment, but I knew I was going down a path that I did not like, living a reality I did not want. I needed to stop it, as it disgusted me watching myself become this person. But I kind of felt trapped and didn't know where to start because I had not been shown any other way to live. After I became aware of this tendency, I found I would notice I had acted out this trait the day after, and I would beat myself up about it, hating the fact that I had stepped back into this place. Then the next time I would notice five minutes after I had done it – once again, beating myself up for playing victim or casting blame when I did not need to. Then the next time, I noticed while I was doing it, and tried to make myself stop, but for some reason, I couldn't. The words just kept pouring out of me. Then, finally, I recognised this before I opened my mouth. I could see where I was headed and stopped it from happening. This is when I broke this hardwired pattern, purely through awareness.

It is so easy to follow in your parental figures' footsteps when that's all you know. It took guts to stand up and question my behaviours, and purely through the awareness of this playing out in my life, I stopped this toxic trait. I found awareness was the key to all my growth and healing. Once I was aware of a wound, belief or behaviour, I started the healing process. Obviously, there are many ways to heal from things, but I have found healing can occur purely through my awareness. When unaware, I keep reacting, just like when I was identifying with my ego – every interaction is a reaction. Awareness is the primary aspect of my growth. If I am not aware, I am asleep.

***

When I had been aware of my spiritual awakening for a little while and what a profound shift in consciousness I embodied, I became aware that everything I was doing was a spiritual practice, and I started to see a lot of myself in those around me. I was becoming aware of my being in every interaction I had. Observing people who are deeply entrenched within their ego allowed me to see certain behaviours in myself. When in social situations or whilst in a state of doing, such as talking or interacting with others, I noticed I needed to become aware of my state of being. When engaging with others, my awareness was key. This prevented ego reactions. I find it far too easy to purely react without thought when I am surrounded by unawakened humans. In the early stages of my awakening, I would continue to have ego-based interactions the majority of the time, until I became aware that I was speaking and reacting from a place of ego. I no longer identified with my ego, so why was I reacting from it when in certain situations? It was because it was still so automatic for me to shape myself around what I think others want to hear or to suit the social situation. Sometimes now, I will interact from a place of ego, but I am always practising and working on this through awareness. I find myself becoming aware of my ego in order to prevent it from creeping back in. It is this awareness that is pivotal to expanding my consciousness.

Awareness is all it takes for me to shift out of ego.

Once consciously awake, I feel it is so important to not engage in spreading unconscious energy and behaviour in my life. Because what's the point in waking up if I continue to be unconscious?

I expanded my awareness to change my life. Awareness is everything.

***

Once I was more aware of my emotions and things that were triggering me, and had become committed to understanding myself on a deeper level, I started to notice how being attached to people, thoughts, outcomes and events was the root of most of my suffering. My attachments affirmed that love, validation and wholeness were lacking from within myself. Attachment was the root of so much of my pain. Attachment to things, people and outcomes often was leaving me feeling unfulfilled and wanting more. I made something that wasn't me, me. I was basing my internal happiness on something external. For example, when I was with my ex-partner, I would change my hair, move my room around or buy some new clothes, and I would get so excited to tell him about it and show him, creating this idea in my head of how it would go when telling him, and I held onto it, replaying it in my mind throughout the day until I finally saw him and told him. I was so attached to this unrealistic idea of how he would react, that if his reaction didn't meet my expectations, I would instantly feel disappointed, and all my feelings of excitement faded. Almost every single time I planned how something was 'meant to go' in my head, I was left feeling unfulfilled. I didn't leave space for the unknown to come in and knock my socks off with something better than excepted because I couldn't even see if something better for me was right in front of my eyes. I was so damn attached to this perfect plan in my head, which is never how life actually goes anyway.

Being attached to people's opinions was another thing that often left me feeling low. If someone didn't like me, I did not like me. If someone didn't have the same opinion as me, I believed that maybe my opinion was wrong. If someone viewed me in a certain way, I became attached to this, and believed what they thought was me and a reflection of me. These were the stories I was telling myself and I would start to question my view. I was too attached to others' opinions to be validated and valued within myself.

I needed to change the stories I was telling myself. Being attached to the outcome of something doesn't leave space for something better. 'This is how it is meant to go,' shuts down other possibilities. A huge one for me was being attached to the idea of what my future was going to look like if I stayed with my ex. He was promising me the world, painting the picture of my ideal life. I was so attached to this that my current reality was blurred. I kept visualising this future and I didn't even consider that my future could be much brighter than the one I had attached myself to within my ego mind. And that's why the universe sent it crumbling down. The universe had to crush this attachment to show me that the life I thought I wanted for myself was so small compared to what the universe had planned for me. Even whilst writing this book, I set a goal for myself to write 1000 words a day. I thought this would benefit me and keep me on track towards my goal of finishing this book during this six-week isolation. Now I find myself getting attached to wanting to achieve this word count each day, and when I don't reach this word count, I start doubting my ability to write and finish this book. I have become attached to the word count and, in turn, created the belief that my ability to write this book is measured by if I can hit this 1000 words each day. Which is ridiculous, but I am aware of this now, and have put a stop to it. Awareness is key. Because now I am aware of this, I can tell myself a different story to the one that's playing out in my subconscious.

Sometimes I still struggle with attachment when manifesting or trying to invite something in. Getting attached to the 'how' of what I want appearing and how it's going to come into my life, what it's going to look like, *blah, blah, blah*. I am learning more and more each day to let go of the 'how' my best life is going to happen, and just visualise it, without being attached. I know it sounds confusing, but to manifest something you want – as I've been told and researched – being within the energy of having already achieved this is the key, by letting go of the attachment to 'how' this will happen. The universe is always surprising us, and if we have an idea as to how something is going to happen for us, we block out the guidance we receive from the universe that is pointing us in the direction of what we want. We can so easily dismiss this guidance as it doesn't look how we are attached to it looking. Therefore, we block it out.

Now when I do find myself getting attached to an outcome, or attached to something that I want to happen, or getting attached to what is next for me in life, I bring myself back to the now, back to the current moment, and I ask myself, *What would make me happiest right now?* Then that attachment to the future is suddenly gone. Coming back to the present moment has been so beneficial for me in many ways. Because I am now aware of attachment and the stories I tell myself, I work on changing this story. I work on changing what I believe.

I was attached to my past with my mum too. So instead of seeing the past as something that hurt me, I changed the story, ensuring I release this attachment. My past doesn't define or manipulate my future. I held so much hate and anger against my mum for things that happened, but the more I understood my conditioning and created awareness around my own trauma,

I realised she was only acting through her own unhealed trauma, and the anger instantly faded away. I started to feel sorry for her. I also no longer felt anger around any situation in my life that caused me grief in the past. I found I was looking at everything in a much different way, reframing the past. I sense my mum has a lot of unspoken trauma she has experienced in her life. I feel the way she acts is a reflection of what is raising within her. I feel my mother goes through phases of briefly waking up, when all her hurt attempts to crack her open. However, the shadow work and pain then overwhelms her, causing her to retract back into the ego mind, go back to sleep and continue to drown the sorrows. Staying strong through the prevention of feeling emotions. The more I talk to my parents, the more I can comprehend their actions, and the more I understand why they act the way they do. They are purely acting through their beliefs and conditioning, like most of us prior to waking up. Dad was also under so much pressure when my parents were still together – pressure to find money, running a business and then coming home to the drama that filled our home – no wonder he would yell the house down. He was angry, just like I was.

I hold no anger, blame or resentment towards anyone or anything that hurt me, which is a perk of awakening, and my relationship with my parents has improved vastly! I am working on my wounds, and it feels so good to forgive. I realise my parents were only acting through their conditioning and I don't hold any blame against them. My parents are incredible people; there are just aspects of them that I struggled with and I am not here to write about all the good times I experienced because I don't feel like the good times pushed me into my awakening.

***

Life isn't about defining who I am, or finding my purpose through career pathways, or painting a picture of who I want to become. It is about unlearning the limiting beliefs I unconsciously tell myself daily that prevent true freedom. I am already whole.

Little Life Update

I just did the most powerful meditation with the intention to receive guidance around this book. The vision I received was of my higher self, my ancestors and my spirit guides surrounding me in one giant group hug. I felt they were all with me, standing by my side, guiding me and channelling messages through me to be placed in this book. It was such a beautiful vision. I feel so much love and support from the divine along this writing journey.

21

Spiritual Awakening Challenges

For a very long time, I struggled with self-love. At the start of my journey, I couldn't even name one thing I liked about myself as it felt so uncomfortable, but I set the task to name two things I loved about myself daily, and it shifted my view on myself. Instead of speaking to myself negatively, I looked for positives, which feels amazing, changing my beliefs about myself. I felt I couldn't love myself around others because I didn't want to be perceived as cocky, self-centred or arrogant in another person's eyes, so for a long time, this held me back from fully embracing the real me. Which is so sad because when we love and appreciate ourselves, it doesn't come from a place of ego, the way others most likely will perceive it, but comes from a place of love and acceptance. Living in love and acceptance is all you could want when you are on the path of raising your vibration and living a soul-filled life. The struggle of dealing with how people perceived me during this period of awakening is something that hit deep to my core. I didn't feel like my old self, but I also didn't feel like I had stepped into a new self yet. I was just different – in a 'limbo' kind of phase, I'll call it – struggling to love who I was becoming, without coming across as cocky.

This awakening was an extremely uncomfortable and challenging thing to navigate for me, and I hope this book will help you through your awakening, giving you some clarity around the challenging times. I felt so many internal changes happening to me and I really struggled with how I would reflect them on the outside. How would I embrace this growth and my new interests without making myself seem so esoteric and just plain weird? I was, honestly, terrified as I put such high value around how others viewed me, only showing the world certain snapshots and what I felt suited the image I was going for at that particular time, or trying only to show people my happiest self.

I worried if others liked me. I would always try to show my best, warm, friendly self. Before my awakening, I like to think I was the kind of person that got along with anyone, because I shaped myself and adapted to whatever social situation presented itself to me. Dwindling away at my own values and self in the process.

My heavy party days lasted about three months. One of my girlfriends and I were running absolutely wild and having a blast. I thought for some time that I could continue to go out and do my spiritual work to raise my vibration during the week, but I realised that wasn't the case at all. I knew if I wanted to grow and be the person I envisioned, I needed to stop it altogether. I was really struggling with this decision as my closest friend at the time wanted to keep going out. She wasn't done with her little partying journey, but I sure was. I knew I needed to stop this in order to grow. I just didn't know how to do it without disappointing her. I felt so much pressure. I wanted to keep her happy and be the party friend she needed at this time, as she was struggling with a break-up too, but I wanted to entirely remove myself from the situation and escape. I felt this overwhelming pull to dive 100% into my spiritual path. I had to do what was best for me. I had so much fear around telling her how I felt, mainly because I felt like I was letting her down, and the last thing I ever wanted to do was let her down. When I finally said that I didn't want to do drugs anymore, she was very supportive with her words, but I could feel (empath life) that she wasn't the happiest about it, as she was losing her wild gal pal. We drifted from this point on. I made the decision to put a stop to this phase right before Victoria was forced into lockdown due to coronavirus, so I wasn't even tempted with a 'good time' because we couldn't do anything or go out anywhere – how perfect.

A few months after this decision to cut party drugs out of my life completely, my birthday was rolling around, in July of 2020, during coronavirus lockdown, which I was actually so relieved about as I didn't want to go out and be put in the situation of feeling like I needed to 'get wild' because it was my birthday. But, of course, that would all be too easy and, of course, the damn universe wanted to test me, to see if I was actually serious about this. So, even though it was completely illegal due to the Covid restrictions at the time, I let my friend throw me a party at one of our mate's places in the middle of nowhere. Now, I knew straight away that at this party there would be drugs floating around. The whole month leading up to the party, I was stressing out. I didn't want to feel the pressure of taking drugs. My ego almost got the better of me. My ego wanted to 'have the most fun' because it was my birthday. My ego wanted to take drugs because it wanted to 'show everyone I'm still fun'. I managed to fully step out of my ego this night – this was a huge test and, damn, it felt good to pass it. It felt so good to feel that growth and stand within my authentic soul-aligned truth! I just had a few too many alcoholic beverages instead. I'm still in lockdown at this time, so I haven't had any other opportunities come up to test me. However, I don't feel like this will be a test again. I have shifted out of my ego now and these friendships. More than ever before, and I am completely content in the new me. I am completely content with my current path and no longer feel the need to please anyone. I made the choice to change my life, chasing my spiritual self, and I haven't touched party drugs since and I don't think I ever will again.

During the early days of my awakening, I really struggled with friendships, and I feel this was definitely due to my beliefs around these friendships and my lack of understanding as to what was happening to me. Especially during my hermit phase, this is when I struggled the most. I felt like no one understood me, and all I wanted to do was retreat to the comfort of my home to be all alone. I pushed almost everyone away at this time. I felt left out and this was really difficult for me. I wanted to be alone, but then when everyone would hang out without me, I would get upset about it. I spent most of the time thinking, *What is wrong with me?* Then I realised these people were no longer in vibrational resonance with me. I was growing, shifting and stepping into a higher consciousness. Growing up, I had always put such high value around my friendships. I love my closest pals and always had this strong belief that friendships were 'forever'. I felt if a close friendship didn't last forever, then I had failed. Which sounds ridiculous now that I think about it, but that was just an unconscious belief I had, most likely picked up from my childhood years, from a movie or something, as commonly beliefs are. During my awakening, I felt myself drifting from friendships that had been in my life since I was a child. I struggled with these people as I was stuck in a limbo phase between who I was and who I was becoming, and I could tell they didn't know how to react to the me I was presenting to them. As I had shifted, certain pastimes – *cough*, party drugs, *cough* – weren't going to be a part of my future and the life I wanted. I wanted to be fully committed to becoming my best self and living my best life. I no longer resonated with these people and they no longer resonated with me. I didn't understand why this was happening and hated it. I wanted so badly to connect with them and open them up to all the 'spiritual stuff', but I realised you cannot force people into this way of life. Sometimes people aren't meant to wake up in this life, and maybe not even in their next. I needed to bring my focus back onto my path and stop forcing myself into situations that were draining me.

I knew that I had gone through a huge shift into my awakening. I knew I had changed and grown in ways I struggled to explain to those around me, but they could see the change within me reflecting to the outside. Causing me to start seeing more of the shadows, which I had blocked out for many years, around many of my relationships. Jealously from others was beginning to arise the more I stepped into my fullest expression. As the light you shine when raising your vibe can cast shadows on areas in another person's life and they can become triggered by you. I learnt during this time how hard it can be to follow your highest good when those around you try and tear you down. Noticing that even some of the closest people around me didn't want to see me grow and succeed, was making me question things more. Some became threatened and resentful as I chased my soul lead path. The bonds that were once there had been severed and I was holding onto a vibrational mismatch and lower state that I was trying so hard to rise from. I felt I had changed, but why should this change cause a loss friendships I'd had for years? I never believed that certain friendships would end, and this really messed with my ego, as I believed friendships were 'forever'. I started to question my beliefs – maybe friendships aren't a lifelong thing? Maybe as we grow and shift, so do our friendships? I forced these relationships for some time. I made the extra effort to spend more time with friends, to talk about things that we used to talk about and to try to keep the friendship alive. Guess what I found? I was no longer enjoying myself and these friendships prevented me from becoming who I wanted to be. I was draining my energy and felt like when I left the environment, I needed to work hard to get my vibe going again to where it was when I started the day. Sometimes I tried to be an extrovert to compensate for the awkwardness I felt around others; this awkwardness came from me pushing against my boundaries. Naturally, I am an introvert. Trying to be an extrovert drained me immensely, but I never realised this. I am now learning how to embrace my introvert side and following what's in alignment with who I am becoming. So, I let some relationships drift away organically. I didn't make it a point to end the friendships; I just drifted away. Honouring myself in the process.

A pivotal part of my growth during this time was when I accepted the fact that I was outgrowing lower vibrational environments, including jobs and people. It was a challenge, but I stopped putting up so much resistance, choosing growth and myself over company. To put it simply, as I raised my vibration, I outgrew things that fit me previously. Knowing when to leave was vital, and I could feel it on an energy level. It felt uncomfortable being around certain people. I no longer felt good around them, and that's okay. I'm not saying I'm better than anyone else or above them, because that's not the case at all. We are all equal. But energy-wise, I had purely outgrown so many people. For example, say you've been working at a local café while studying to become a nurse. Once you've finished studying and gained the knowledge you need to move into the role as a nurse, you do. You leave the café as it doesn't resonate with where you want to be. It was the same with friendships, jobs and everything within my life. Things were constantly shifting due to my internal shifts. At the start of my spiritual awakening, I lost myself, and my friends. I could no longer work a 'normal job' and my family thought I was on crack. *This was livin'.*

Others didn't drift away as easily and kept coming back into my life, stunting my growth. I realised that as I continue to grow as a person, I need to surround myself with the kind of energy that I want to be, and this required strength. A common theme around this spiritual lifestyle is that people in higher vibe states don't allow lower vibes around them – they don't even allow that energy in their space. Now, this isn't me saying that some people are less and some are better, but it's just a fact that everyone is at a different stage in their journey. Some people are living in lower states and are still spending their time complaining and gossiping, which they may choose to do forever, and this is totally okay. So, it seems obvious that hanging around this is going to rub off on me. Of course, I struggled to grow whenever I hung out with certain people, as I was brought back down to where I was previously, vibrationally. In some cases, I needed strength to lovingly remove or block these energies out of my life, creating boundaries. I did feel guilt and some lack of trust within myself around whether this was the right thing, which made it harder to extricate myself. I found it easier when I focused not on what I was losing, but instead on the high vibe state I would continue to delve into, giving myself a happier life. Remember – quality energy over quantity.

It sucked losing friends, but that's just the reality when you decide to level up and choose a better path, so I changed my perspective to creating space for new relationships to come in. After sitting with myself and my emotions, I decided to give myself a card reading on one lonely night. I received the card 'call in your tribe'. I thought to myself, *What does that even mean? I struggle to connect with my closest mates like I used to?* Then it clicked. I needed to meet new people who were more in alignment with where I was at along my journey. I couldn't believe I didn't think of this earlier on, but I was also thinking, *How do I even meet people who are going through an awakening?* I didn't exactly want to make a post online: *Ummm, hey, guys. I'm going through a spiritual awakening and I'm into all the esoteric shizz. I stay awake at all hours watching weird vids on YouTube. I've lost my friends. My family thinks I'm nuts ... Do you like this stuff? Do you wanna be my friend? Haha*, could you imagine? So as any sane person would do, I asked my spirit guides out loud to bring me my soul family – I was calling them in. The next day, I had a card reading with a beautiful chick, Millie, as at this stage, I was offering intuitive card readings online. I had a feeling as soon as I jumped on that video call that she was more than just a usual reading. As we got chatting, I was thinking, *This is the kind of person I want to be friends with.* We just got along so damn well, and everything just flowed. Long story short – a few months on, Millie is my absolute soul sister! We 100%, no doubt in our minds, have known each other in past lives! We have similar interests and goals! We have both been through our awakening and we are currently at similar phases in our lives too, both raising our vibration together, supporting and guiding each other along the way! We are both committed to growth and this spiritual path and that is all I could have ever hoped for in a soul sister! We have met for a reason, and without her support, I don't think this book would have happened, as I didn't have the confidence that all this gibberish I go on about could actually help people until Millie and I connected. I am so incredibly grateful to have met her! Thank you, spirit guides! Love you big time.

So a valuable lesson I have learnt during this whole journey of awakening is that friendships do not need to last a lifetime. Recognise when a friendship, job or relationship is over and let it go, or learn how to create healthy boundaries. I allow myself to gracefully remove myself from situations that no longer allow me the space to grow and flourish. I have not failed if a relationship doesn't prosper for years. Sometimes relationships briefly appear for a season to teach me things, to help me grow along the way. Losing people created space for my soul family to walk into my life. Release and surrender to the universe.

***

I feel when I raise my vibration more and more, I need to readjust my boundaries. What was okay before, no longer works, as I have shifted into an entirely new state of being. The people in my life, my self-care rituals and the environments I surround myself with must meet my new vibrational frequency in order to be sustained, and this can be challenging. I would violate my boundaries far too often in the past, by people-pleasing, spending time doing things I did not want to, and by not speaking up when something bothered me or was important to me. My balance of giving and receiving was out of whack. I would give far too often, not allowing myself to receive. I did not make my own energy a priority, and I didn't know how to recognise my limits and would burn myself out frequently. Creating boundaries and learning to say no to things that no longer resonate were vital to my growth and energy. People-pleasing went out the window. I became aware that people-pleasing, putting others before myself, is linked to low self-worth. I learnt how to ask myself what it was that I wanted. This was foreign to me as I had never really done this before. Some guilt would creep in, but I became aware of it and pushed past it. I have finally invited in the fact that there is nothing wrong with looking after me. If another person chooses to be unhappy due to my actions of placing myself first, that is their decision to feel that way. They have the power to choose the way they create their lives, as I am now doing. Honestly, stepping up and getting your shit together requires so much guts. You need to own up to your shit, release what and who no longer serve you, and realise that you are the only one holding yourself back.

Let go, so you can flow. Release and call in your soul family!

***

I feel like this whole spiritual awakening thing would be so much easier to go through if I was living alone. Being an empath and highly intuitive made living with my family a struggle. This was some lower energy I couldn't remove. Living with my dad, who enjoys complaining and living in the negative state, sometimes made it hard to keep my vibe high. To help, I imagine myself covered and surrounded in white light, which blocks out the lower energy. I also don't contribute to lower vibe exchanges, such as conversation that doesn't make me feel good, and I lovingly remove myself.

The fam started to notice that something was up with me, but when I tried to explain to them what was happening, they would get all confused and think I had lost the effing plot. Imagine living with people who are worried about your strange new ways, so you try to keep your old self on show so you don't worry them, all whilst diving into the new witchy you as soon as your bedroom door is closed. Luckily for me, my awakening hit shortly after my break-up, so my family just put it down to me being a heartbroken chick in her early twenties 'having a moment' and 'finding herself' and 'needing space'. So, all too often, I'd find myself retreating back to the comfort of my room, where I could embrace my inner hippie in somewhat peace. I say *somewhat* because if you know my dad, you'll know his voice is so bloody loud that the whole street knows when I need to unstack the dishwasher. His loud voice triggers me so hard, and I found it particularly difficult during the early days of my awakening as I didn't understand how to protect my energy just yet, and I was so sensitive to noise, I couldn't even listen to my old favourite rap tunes without feeling super uncomfortable. I was feeling so sensitive at this time that whenever my dad was home, I would pray for him to go around to his girlfriend's place so I could spend my nights meditating and diving into some past-life regression sessions without interruption. I just needed some peace. Dad thought I was asking him to leave some nights because I wanted to have boys over. Really, I just wanted to trip out on some past-life stuff in peace.

For some time, I was worried that living with my family would hinder my growth, as I couldn't have peace 24/7 and live in a constant state that's not in this world, as I like to put it. I needed to shift this mindset as it would create a self-fulfilling prophecy, and I didn't really need to be alone 24/7 – I was just being my hermit self, living in extreme comfort. If I believed living at home would hinder my growth, then it would, so I changed my mindset and embraced living with my family and this stage of my life. I have grown in other ways. I have learnt how to block out unwanted sound, and how to keep peace within myself even when my dad's voice is bellowing around the house. The best thing I did to help was removing myself from the house when everyone's energy just got too much. I was so sensitive, it was almost unbearable. Going for a walk always helped, or a drive – anything to escape. I also found that making my room a space of tranquillity helped tremendously. Keeping my room clean and having candles burning made the space feel nice. I also never let anyone in my room, keeping it purely my space and my energy. I'm excited to see what shifts and growth I will experience once I move out of home. I am manifesting my dream home – stay tuned.

Unawakened people would trigger the absolute fuck out of me in the early days of my awakening. I found that my ego had stepped out of the building, and a new spiritual ego had snuck in the back door. I found myself no longer wanting to surround myself with unawakened people and my spiritual ego had me thinking I was above this, which was silly, as the majority of the people in my life are not awake. I would commonly feel drained, and upset and I would start to get angry at myself for falling into the unconscious trap of reaction when around them – it is so easy for me to become unconscious when around the unconscious. Now, it would be easy if I could wake everyone up, but that's not the case, and I don't need to do that. I just needed to shift my perspective and become aware when the spiritual ego is stepping in the back door. I started to think back to when I was asleep, unconscious, completely unaware, and had no idea that I was living a life manipulated by my autopilot thoughts. We are just at different stages on our journeys. I needed to remember that I am no better than people who are unconscious to their souls. I was unconscious at one stage too.

***

I am gifted self-discovery through challenges.

Little Life Update

Tonight, I was scrolling online and a medium I have followed for quite some time was 'live'. I have never really watched 'lives' online before but, for some reason, I was drawn to this one. I clicked on and started watching – he was giving psychic readings to his followers. I requested a reading and I just knew I was going to get selected to join his video. My intuition was on point, so I quickly got up from the couch and rushed to my room. As I was rushing, I got connected to the 'live'! Out of hundreds of people, I was selected! I knew my guides had put this on my path for a huge boost of the motivation I needed. He told me during my reading that I was 'the phoenix that does rise from the ashes', that I needed to 'push past self-doubt', 'people want to hear my story', I'm having an 'eat pray love moment', a 'blooming moment', 'transformation', and that I needed to 'get my butt into gear'. These messages were heard loud and clear. After having that reading, it gave me the motivation my lazy ass needed to keep going. I found it so easy to be lazy and let self-doubt take over from getting the book flowing. My notes in my phone would continue to grow as I write down everything that channels through me during each day but opening my laptop some days just didn't happen. I have never committed myself to something like this before, and having faith that I'm on the right path hasn't always been easy. It is so incredibly powerful how the universe always gifts me exactly what I need, when I need it.

22

In Touch with My Higher Self

Today, my dad asked about this little book of mine. 'What's it about?' 'How do you get it published?' I've been pondering the getting-it-published thing all afternoon. How will I get this creation of mine published? I guess I never really thought about that before. In the past, I would have let this little detail eat away at me and probably would have given up. Actually, I most definitely would have talked myself out of writing this book altogether. Prior to this, I was blindly trusting the universe – you know, trusting the process – and as I write this, I'm realising, having trust within the universe is all I could ever have hoped for! This realisation flooded my heart centre with warmth!

Woo-hoo! Unrealised growth!

That's the beauty of writing things down – it helps me tap

into my subconscious mind and my higher self. Writing allows me to flow deeper and understand, more than any thought process can. Writing allows me to tap into soul messages. When in flow, I become aware. I unravel and I heal myself from the inside, reflecting back into my 3D reality. Journaling is the single most healing practice I could have ever implemented into my life. It's an indescribable energy release, each word dissolving the clouds from my mind and revealing the light of my soul. Whenever I felt stuck, lonely, confused, or my mind was running one million miles an hour, I journaled. This changed my life and this is why so many people preach it in the spiritual community. In the past, I would think to myself, *I am not journaling. What the hell is journaling going to do? I don't even know where to start. Blah, blah, blahhhh.* Simply picking up a pen and writing on a piece of paper has truly given me so much clarity. I use journal prompts to get started. Some days, I allow some time to sit down and fully delve into journaling. Some days, I feel difficulty at the start, battling with my ego mind, pushing past the ego and getting into a state free of judgement and expectations, letting my soul guidance flow. I also found journaling a great way to keep track of how much I have grown and healed along the way. Some days, I look back at pages I have written only a few months prior and I feel like I'm reading something written by a completely different person. It is incredible – journaling has helped me to understand my awakening journey and myself on a level I could have never dreamed of. Honestly, there's nothing quite as beautiful as getting to know your higher self.

***

As I became more familiar with my intuition, I started to get tested by my higher self. I believe our higher self is our eternal consciousness, an intelligent being who is one's self. When we come to earth, we forget the eternal souls we are; awakening is when we start to remember. I first started to recognise that I was getting tested by my higher self after my relationship ended. Incredible timing. I was already a mess. The last thing I wanted was a test. I was receiving so many signs and had that inner knowing it was time to leave the relationship. I had outgrown it. However, once I left, all the signs stopped, my intuition was cut off and it was like I had taken this huge leap and my intuition just left me there alone, falling in silence. I needed to trust.

It's super ironic and has been confusing when my higher self decides to test me. It seems like something has gone wrong. I easily lose my connection to my intuition, sometimes even lapsing into old patterns. As I got further along into my awakening, I found my higher self was testing me more often. I went through these challenges, thinking, in my case, instantly, that things were going wrong because I was on the wrong path. But there is no such thing as the wrong path. We are always exactly where we need to be on the journey of transformation. I started to recognise these tests from my higher self. They often came up as little hurdles, past lessons resurfacing, intuition cut off – all the signs I had previously been receiving up until I took a leap stopped. My clear guidance stopped. I had the inner knowing that I was pushed here for a reason! This tested my faith and belief in myself and my intuition, whereas when I was doing something not in alignment, I clearly felt it within my body.

These tests weren't things going badly wrong; they were more little hits to test my commitment. Getting into my power, persevering and learning to trust my intuition has shown me that I am ready to be challenged and ready to be taken to the next level.

Which brings me to today. Today, my higher self gave me a good old test and many lessons within this, which I understand now, but I'm still feeling uncomfortable about it. I feel personally victimised by my higher self. Yes, I know, I need to shut up and be grateful. I received a psychic reading from a lady online, and after I got off the call, all I could think was, *What the actual fuck was that? Hahaha.* I got myself so wound up because of the things she said, I can't believe it. The thing that got me the most wound up was that this lady had mentioned that my spirit guides were telling her, 'No, you shouldn't write this book,' and I'm like, 'HOLD UP, BITCH. WHAT? I'm 30,000 words in, having a blast because I feel like this is my soul's purpose, flowing with ease and light, and my guides are telling me not to write this damn book?! *Wtf.* I started to question why. Then it hit me. *Is this a test? Surely this isn't a test? Why would my higher self test me now?* I thought I was confident that this is what I'm meant to do, and this is exactly why I got tested. I so easily started to doubt my path based off what some online psychic had said to me.

As I write this, I'm feeling like a dumb bitch, so easily trusting of others' abilities. And, look, maybe my guides did say that to her – *maybe* – and they were communicating the test from my higher self, but, seriously, I did need this test. Over the past few days, I have been writing more consistently than ever before, and really pushing myself to make the time to write every day, because on the weekend, I gave myself a little reading and the cards reflected that I need to be more disciplined. I took that as making time to write, as opposed to just writing when I had the time and really felt like it. The damn lesson and test was to trust myself! No one else should be able to tell me whether or not I should write this book, and I feel stupid for even letting this reading take that confidence away from me. This is my soul's purpose, this is going to help so many people and I am here for it! I am rocking up! No test is going to stop me! Actually, that just reminded me – my cousin said to me jokingly during our family Zoom catch-up today (Covid-19 life), 'Would anyone even want to read that book?' I shrugged it off and didn't even think about it again until now – another little test. Of course, people will want to read this. It's going to change lives. *Duh.* See how when I start to recognise these little tests and show up to the challenge, I come out the other side stronger and more aligned than ever before? I stepped up, and I can feel this within my heart centre right now – this is what I'm meant to do.

***

With deep suffering comes deep transformation.

23

A Whole New Identity

I had a feeling I was so close to finding what I was meant to do, even though I was so lost and everything was falling apart. My career that I was once so passionate about no longer felt like it was a match for me energy-wise. I was getting waves of passion around this whole spiritual healer life. I was being guided to let go of big things in my life, like my long-term relationship. I was growing fast, constantly revaluating friendships, career and life in general, and nothing felt stable. It was all crumbling down. I asked my guides to show me the way and I set the intention!

In the lowest of times during the early days of my awakening, realising how unhappy I was, I started to question why I was so scared to step into my truest self. Like, who cares what the fuckers around me think? Wouldn't I rather live my most authentic life? Wouldn't I rather be happy? Feeling the way I did at that time was not how I wanted to live my life. I was riddled with fear and anxiety, and, quite frankly, I was sick of my own bullshit. I needed to trust these niggling feelings and throw fear aside, to step into my most authentic life.

I was tired of settling for mediocre in my life all because I feared change, so eight months ago, I took a leap. I threw fear aside and put myself out there on the big scary online world. One of the most useful things I ever did to push past fear was whipping out my journal and writing down what I would do if fear didn't exist. What would I do if I didn't give a flying fuck about what Tom down the road thought? What would I do if I didn't have anything stopping me? What would I do if all the things that could possibly go wrong didn't exist or there was no option of that happening? What would I do if the universe had my back and money wasn't an issue? I asked myself these questions! I also wrote down all the positive outcomes that could occur if I didn't let fear hold me back. I pictured the life I could have once I stepped into my purpose! I imagined how amazing everything would turn out once I took that step towards fear! If you haven't already noticed, I am a creative mind; visualisation is a game changer for me! I started sharing and posting things I was interested in online, letting my inner hippie fly, and hoping that sharing certain topics would help those around me on their own paths.

Drowning in fear, I posted an offering of intuitive card readings for free to people online during the early days of Covid, hoping this would be a nice little support for those who needed it. I was receiving such an incredible response, I felt like it was in perfect alignment with me, and I was feeling such high vibes,

I couldn't believe I let fear hold me back for so long. I was so happy. I felt alive! Pushing past fear is a rush! This was the answer to my prayers. I knew I was on track to finding my purpose. I could see it, travelling, connecting with people, and catching some rays. I was flowing with such ease. Everything was working out amazingly. I was finally following my inner guidance! Gee, it felt good! Not long after posting my card readings online and offering them to the big scary world, I felt a strong pull to help others to become the happiest version of themselves, to follow their own spiritual journey, become the best version of themselves and start loving life again! Initially, I was terrified and hesitant. I wasn't sure exactly how I was going to share my knowledge with people, and if they would even take me seriously. I was scared people would doubt my knowledge and I was starting to doubt my knowledge (thanks, fear). All I knew was that I wanted to help others! My soul was calling for it and I needed to trust the process, so that's exactly what I did. Every time fear tried to sneak in again, I would push it aside! Some days, it was almost unbearable. I wanted to give up, and stay in that place of comfort where nothing but unfulfilled dreams lived, but I pushed past the fear of what others thought and kept charging ahead!

I felt pulled to create a one-on-one coaching program. I wanted to work closely with people, utilising my counselling skills and being the high vibe support others needed along their journey. The Raise Your Vibe program was for anyone wanting to set up the foundations for lifelong growth and needing support along their journey. This program provides the support and guidance needed to change lives in a positive way. I support my clients via a messaging app during the week. The program includes weekly lessons, weekly Intuitive Guidance Coaching Sessions via video call, weekly Intuitive Card Reading, and Journaling prompts. We tap into the beliefs people reinforce in themselves in everyday life and create awareness around any blocks, internal conflicts, limiting beliefs and patterns of behaviour, because, remember, awareness is key.

My Raise Your Vibe program consists of daily practices to implement, creating awareness and feeding the soul. We implement daily gratitude to start every day off in a high vibrational state. Then we learn about vibration and how we need to be aware that everything we do is either going to raise your vibe or lower it. Next, heart-brain connection. When we tune in to our heart, we are connecting to a unified field. The heart is centre-focused, so when we tune in to our heart centre, we don't have the mind interfering. This is why it is extremely common in many spiritual teachings to feel from our heart centre for what is in alignment with us. Grounding our energy by walking barefoot outside, or even just by sitting or working outdoors, electrically reconnects us to the earth. These charges from the earth can have positive effects on your body and vibrational energy; therefore, raising our vibration even higher.

Then I teach all about beliefs. We need to become aware of the beliefs and stories we tell ourselves subconsciously, as they are the ego mind trying to keep us in a lower state of vibration. Then we recognise that we are separate to our minds. In fact, I feel the greatest key to raising our vibration is by observing our thoughts and disconnecting from them. We create a meditation routine. Meditation is a key component of creating inner peace.

It is also an incredible way to receive soul messages. Meditation has aided in silencing my mind. I am forever grateful for this practice; it truly changed my life. Lastly, we visit the flow state. When we get into a flow state, time no longer exists, and we flow with passion. Your flow state may be dancing, painting or reading – it could be anything. My flow state recently has been writing this book. Some days, I'll sit down, and before I know it, four hours have passed and it doesn't even feel like twenty minutes.

I created this program because when I was in the darker phases of my awakening, I would have killed for something like this. I craved support and guidance along this journey. I would have loved something to refer back to and tell me what I needed to do every day to become happier and get through this time, as I was stuck in a lower state hunting for guidance. I never want someone else to feel the way I did. I want to help people feel incredible! To start loving life and to feel amazing! And the way we do this is by raising our vibrational state! This program gets people excited for this spiritual life and I am there along the way for support! After week one of completing daily gratitude, I can feel the energy shift within the people in my program – it's incredible.

Around the halfway mark is usually when I start to feel a greater shift in consciousness from those involved, like they take a huge leap into their new self, as this is when we separate ourselves from our mind and can choose to no longer identify with our toxic thought patterns causing a lower vibrational behaviour and reality. This stage is when people start to become immensely grateful as they cannot believe that they once identified with their minds and were running on autopilot around 90% of the time. It honestly blows my mind how much this program has helped people so far, and I keep having moments when I'm thinking, *Damn, I wish my book was finished. It would really help this person.* I feel I need to reach more people, and this book is the way to do it. I have stepped into my purpose! This is it! I am overflowing with love and gratitude! Raising my vibe has changed my life for the better. I have a much higher set point, so the bad days are never as bad as they were before. It does not matter how bad things appear in my external world, I sit comfortably and secure within my internal world, embracing my power, knowing I can face anything. This little program has shown me my purpose – I am here to connect with and heal others.

I never thought my journey of self-discovery, helping and healing myself would end up helping others in the way it has, but this is what I am here to do. I am currently running this program and I am loving it. It's funny, though – I created this program to help people gain a greater understanding of themselves and their reality, which it does and is having a profound impact on the people who have taken a leap. However, surprisingly, I've found since running this program, I am gaining a vast amount of knowledge around my own awakening and the phases I unknowingly experienced. This program is giving me more wisdom and understanding of things I have popped into this book. Win, win. The universe works in mysterious ways.

The crazy part of all this is that the fear I had was entirely made up in my mind. My friends, family and even people online had started to say that I was 'glowing' and happiness was radiating from within me. Pushing past fear invited in my purpose! Any step towards fear is a step towards my desired life. Everything I have ever wanted has been on the other side of fear. I feel I'm only just scratching the surface of my life's purpose; I feel it's growing and evolving the more I expand.

Before I started my design business, I never thought I'd have the guts to start a business and actually receive work from it, especially being so young. I learnt during this time that age doesn't mean shit. I was passionate and had the knowledge to back me within the design space, and this little lesson followed through into this book. Also when offering my coaching program, age doesn't mean shit. When I was pondering the idea of writing a book, some things my ego would pop into my mind included: *You're too young to write about your spiritual awakening. Are people even going to take you seriously? Do people even want to hear your story?* I put a stop to that ego straight-up. I am purely here to tell my story, to describe my experiences and the way I perceived them. There has always been a lesson in everything I have been through, pushing me to this moment, and I wasn't going to let fear hold me back. Fear is a huge part of our human experience; fear is the number one thing that held me back for years. Fear of failing, the fear of not being good enough, the fear of what my family thinks, of what my friends think, fear of what random Tom, Dick and Harrys think! Fear held me back from growth and where I wanted to be. With coronavirus putting my design business on hold, I had so much free time, I didn't know what to do with myself. This is when I decided to push past the fear and offer intuitive card readings online for free, as I had nothing else to do and the niggling feeling that I should offer readings just wouldn't stop. Not long after posting my card readings online and offering them to the big scary world, I felt a strong pull to create an e-book, so I did. I also started charging for my card readings and I cannot believe how easily it all came together; I was flowing in true alignment. I had finally figured out that my life's purpose is to be a healer and help others, and this purpose is continually growing and evolving the more I expand.

I realised recently that KYLYN Design is no longer in alignment with my soul's purpose, after two whole years of battling with it. Due to coronavirus, this business is pretty much non-existent currently. I can no longer complete appointments and I have zero cash flow coming in. It's costing me money. Now, in the past, my business crashing and burning would have been my worst nightmare because having this business satisfied my ego. It was a part of my identity. But now? It's funny – I worked so hard to get this business running. I pushed so hard for it, and now that coronavirus has come and stopped it in its tracks, surprisingly, I feel relieved and maybe even happy about it because I know it has pushed me into my real purpose. I still have a passion for design. I love it. I just know I have a greater purpose now. I'm currently stuck in two minds about whether to shut KYLYN Design down. I know I have multiple appointments coming up as soon as this coronavirus lockdown ends, and money-wise, it would be good. However, knowing that this is no longer in alignment, I have this strong pull to shut it down completely. But my mind is telling me that this is a crazy idea. I've worked so hard to get this business going, all to just shut it down because of some niggling feeling I have about some book

I'm writing that might not even get me anywhere? Absolutely bonkers, but that's what this is all about, right? Trusting the universe?

***

I just did a card reading on myself and it's been decided. I've shut it down. Always trust the niggle. Leap. I am so proud of how far I have come along my journey, having this trust within the universe. Even though it may scare the shit out of me, I'm trusting. Also, you know what's funny? As soon as I set the intention to be living in my purpose, surrendered to the universe and stopped chasing, the universe presented my life's purpose to me on a silver platter represented by synchronicities, repetitive thoughts, feelings and signs! I truly feel that writing this book is a part of my purpose, and it is honestly the last thing I ever thought I would do! It's crazy how when I stopped looking to make money and trusted in the divine guidance that was delivered to me, I found my purpose!!!!

24

A New Way of Living

Over the past twelve hours, I've had some major shifts occur, so I'm feeling the need to give you a little life update and this ties in perfectly with the previous chapter. Funny about that (fuckin' universe – got me again). It's currently the 13th of August 2020, and the energy in Melbourne now is intense as we are in week three of a six-week, stage-four Covid-19 lockdown. Being an empath, I have been feeling this energy, feeling drained and overwhelmed. I've also been struggling with being trapped within a 5 km radius from my house. This means no beach. This means an ungrounded, uneasy Shay is hanging around. I've been doing my best to keep my vibes high, going for runs, pumping tunes and dancing around. However, nothing recharges me more than the deep blue sea. Even on the coldest of Melbourne days, you'll find me taking the leap into this ice-cold water to feed my soul and clear my mind.

For the past couple of months, I have been booked-up with card readings and my Raise Your Vibe! I have been feeling over the moon, feeling like I have found my purpose, feeling like, *Yes, this is it! This is what I'm meant to do! Help others! I'm a healer!* Things were flowing all too smoothly. I was waiting for the universe to offer me a situation that was going to test me and put me on a higher level than ever before. Here it is. I have really committed to writing this book, making time for it, as I know this needs to be put into the world. I started to find myself getting really drained from doing card readings, whereas a couple of weeks ago, I would feel alive, buzzing with energy after a reading! I thought I was just getting more and more drained due to the collective energy. However, I started to realise and ponder the idea that maybe my card readings aren't as in alignment with me as they were a few months ago. *Maybe I'm meant to put more energy into my book?* I feel writing isn't draining me. Writing makes me feel alive, as the card readings previously did. This is when my ego and fear stepped in. *Why would you have been guided to pump this card reading thing, only to be feeling it's not in alignment a few short months later?*

As I wrote that, I had the thought that I wouldn't have even started writing this book if I didn't start putting myself and my knowledge out there online. So, noticing this little niggling feeling, I decided to give myself a good old card reading, to gain some clarity around this whole situation. *Why is this happening? Why am I feeling so drained after readings? Why am I getting flooded with things to write in my book during readings where I'm meant to have my entire focus on someone else?* The cards that I received were 'align your life', 'what's not in alignment and needs to change', 'get grounded', and 'pillar of light, your vibration is rising'. Well, well, well, thanks, guides. I knew straight away that the 'align your life' card was relating to giving card readings. This simply wasn't in alignment with me anymore. As much as this sucks, I had to be proud as I have raised my vibration higher and have got myself on a more optimal timeline. Instantly, my ego mind stepped up, telling me that cutting back on readings was going to get me further away from my goals of travelling and buying my dream house, *blah, blah*. My ego mind never makes sense of my soul guidance, so block that out and trust the damn process. I made that sound easier than it is! But seriously! You got this! I have taken the steps, listened to my guidance, and have cut back on intuitive card readings to focus on my book and my Raise Your Vibe program. I am trusting my intuition.

Far out, imagine if this book doesn't get published. *Hahaha.* Wait, stop – this book is going to change lives. See how I just blocked out that fear and flipped it around?

The number one clue that helps me realise something isn't in alignment with me anymore is me getting more drained or frustrated than usual from a particular task, job, person, situation, whatever it is. When I am living out of alignment, my external reality doesn't match up to what I desire. I don't get excited to get out of bed in the morning. I feel disconnected from myself. I feel uninspired, or like I'm letting fear control me. Another sign for me is things keep going wrong. Like, for example, I'm still currently working two days a week part-time to keep money coming in – you know, to pay all those good old bills we all know and love. When I'm at this job, I feel *sooooooooo* drained after, and things just keep going wrong. Last week, my computer wouldn't turn on for hours. Then once it finally decided to turn on, I couldn't connect to the internet, so I literally couldn't get anything done. Then the following day, my computer mouse broke – again, I wasn't able to complete the stack of work piling up, causing me to crack under pressure and call it a day. I ended up going home and writing some pages in this book. Funny how this all works out, isn't it? I do my absolute best to live in alignment.

You don't necessarily need to have trust within yourself. Place your trust in the universe. Universe provides.

Tonight, I find myself sitting in bed on Sunday night flicking through my journal. I realise that only four short months ago, I was hoping and praying to find my life's purpose. I had no idea what truly lit me up and what I wanted to do in this life. On the 7/04/20 on the night of the super full moon, I wrote in my journal and set the intention to invite in my life's purpose. On the 22/04/20, I posted online offering my card readings. A few weeks after that is when I wrote my e-book, and a week after that is when I started my Raise Your Vibe program to help others along their own journeys. AND NOW I'm writing this book! (16/08) AND THE LIGHTS JUST FLICKERED! This is insane! The universe really does have your back when you set some intentions. It is also so important to look back and see how far you have come! I honestly cannot believe that only four months ago I didn't have a clue what my purpose was! Now I will set the intention to move into this life as a full-time career, a career travelling and helping people around the world. Universe, I am inviting this in! I am placing my trust in the universe once more and intend to live in alignment with ease.

Now I have found in the spiritual community, there is a common perception that you don't need 'things' to be happy and you should be happy without 'things'. This whole 'minimal' lifestyle has become trendy recently too. Which I'm all for, but I feel there is that side of things where sometimes we are made to feel guilty for wanting nice things within the spiritual community, or we feel the pressure to offer things such as card reading for free because it is something that we enjoy and should do it for the 'love of it'. Now, I truly believe wanting to live a comfortable and abundant life is something that we should not feel guilty about. We are allowed to have everything we want in life. Money is purely an energy exchange, like anything else in this world. The problem lies in deriving our sense of happiness from things we want, or maybe a better way to put it is 'from things we don't currently have'.

I noticed that my ego was always a split of fear and desire. I wanted things and I was scared of not getting them or not 'making it in life' and I derived my happiness from them. I was afraid I wouldn't obtain financial stability and wanted a life where I could easily build my dream home one day. I became attached to these desires, and unconsciously was telling myself that I would be happy once I achieved whatever it was that I wanted that month. Once I got whatever it was I wanted, there was always the next thing on my mind, and then I never allowed myself to be happy with the other thing I wanted for so long, as I had already moved onto the next. It has become so important to realise when a desire is arising and become aware that this is purely a desire and not something that my happiness is connected to. I no longer place happiness within what I want.

I am already whole, no matter what I have in my external world. It is completely okay to want things! I want things! I would absolutely froff a jet ski! But I don't let myself be unhappy because I don't have a jet ski – do you get what I'm saying? I view this desire from a place of neutrality. I do not need a jet ski. I am whole already. It is so easy to feel unhappy because we haven't got something that we desire in life. The key is to feel happy and whole no matter what 'things' are around you.

***

About three weeks ago, I was in such a state of bliss, I couldn't believe it! I was so content, happy and grateful for my life, I couldn't wipe the smile off my face. I was radiating high vibes and everyone around me could feel it. I felt like a bomb-ass spiritual goddess. I believed I had 'done the work' and had raised my vibration to a point I was happy with. I was overwhelmed with happiness and I never thought it would end. Now let's skip to today. I am thinking back to the me of three weeks ago, and I cannot believe I actually thought I would stay that happy forever. I cannot believe I was so naive to have thought I had done all the inner work and got to a place I was content with. Over the past week and a half, I have been feeling super flat, drained, sort of unmotivated, with weird lower vibrational energy hitting me in weird times for no clear reason. I thought maybe I was getting my period and feeling all those girly emotions but that wasn't it. I was no longer in the overly joyful state I was in a few weeks back. I had no idea what the reason behind this was and, to be honest, over the past couple of days, I've been sick of it. I keep getting tested by the universe and I'm tired, but definitely not giving up. I mean, look at me pushing through this. I could so easily have hopped into bed tonight after work and chucked a movie on, but writing this out has demanded that I discover and understand what is happening. Over the past week, I started seeing the number 243 on number plates, the clock and even job numbers at work. Today on my drive home, I saw this number about four times, so I consulted the book that I use almost every day to look up these repetitive numbers I see all too often, and 243 means: *Don't be alarmed if you are feeling low. You are processing energy in order to raise your vibration.* Then it all started to make sense.

I realised I would go through periods where I found myself in lower vibrational energy right before I stepped into a higher level of consciousness and a higher vibe. I realised that there wasn't anything bringing my mood down from my external reality. However, my body was in a state of processing. I was processing memories and energy in order to raise my vibration. I found during these times of processing, often past hurt will arise in quiet moments. I have learnt to look at this and allow the emotions and energy to pass, not hold onto them, realise the hurt is there, feel it and move on. Also, when past trauma arises, I acknowledge that this is the past and release it – I no longer need to hold on. I found it very easy to let these times of processing get me down as, energy-wise, I do feel down. I remind myself it is normal to feel low before you rise and step higher than ever before. Even just having the awareness (see, back to the good old awareness) and some better clarity around what is happening has enabled me to lift my vibe. I also feel comfort in knowing that a whole new level of contentment is awaiting me.

Processing and releasing these emotions, memories and energy is a vital part of healing. There will be phases, ups and downs, shifts in energy, and this all happens for a reason. Balance is key. I have been learning to find balance between healing, processing, working, fun, friends, family and everything else within life, but the more I try to find balance, the more I realise that losing balance is the reality of life.

We need to process and release to rise.

***

Before my awakening, I realised I was always in a state of doing – doing this, doing that, always on the move, never allowing space for just 'being'. When in the present moment, I am not thinking of the past or the future, not allowing space for the lower vibrational energies such as anxiety, guilt, fear and shame to step in. I have found that these lower states easily creep in when I am thinking about the past, or the future, creating a gap between the present moment and my thoughts and emotions. This was the key to beating my anxiety. In the past, I wasn't present for the majority of my life. My mind was always running wild and I never really embraced the moment I was in. I changed my life when I put my full focus on the now, not worrying about tomorrow, or last week's embarrassing situation.

Some of the ways I bring myself back to the present moment is through sensory perception, noticing my breath, really feeling it. If I'm in a state of doing, I really feel what I'm doing. I put my entire focus on what's happening in front of me, looking at all the tiny details – this is super grounding. Sensory perception is an incredible way to become present.

***

All that really matters is the present moment. Becoming present is our greatest gift.

25

The Good Stuff

Presenting the new me into the world! What a giant leap towards fear this was. One thing that constantly played on my mind was the fact I was going to appear like one of those chicks that go through a break-up and 'find themselves', which is exactly what happened, but I didn't want it to seem like I was being cocky, self-centred or arrogant by presenting my newfound happiness to the world. One of the ways I outed the new me to the people around me was online. I changed my whole look. I started offering card readings. I started posting things I was passionate about. And I started along my path of helping others! Which is something I have always been drawn to. However, societal conditioning and doubt from those around me had caused the counselling route to take a detour, which, in retrospect, is exactly how it needed to happen for me to follow my spiritual and intuitively guided path as opposed to the clinical life.

I dived into fear, embraced my hippie side and told myself that I needed to push through the fear. On the other side of fear is everything I have ever wanted. I found myself pushing through fear and trusting the universal guidance and signs I was being bombarded with. In every little thing in my life, I was being guided and supported! I dressed more 'out there', got myself the car I always wanted, and wrote a damn e-book! I offered card readings online. I studied reiki healing. Everything I never thought I would do, and everything I never thought I would become, I have. And you know the funniest thing that I had never thought of prior to stepping straight into the barrel of fear? I was so blinded by the fear that I couldn't see clearly into possible future turns of events. I couldn't see even a glimmer of positivity on the other side. I purely saw it as me stepping into fear to become my true self. To my utmost surprise, most of the people around me supported me (my craziness), connected with me on a deeper level than ever before and loved watching me discover my passions!

As I write this, I struggle to even comprehend how I was riddled with fear, riddled with how others would perceive me. I will never allow myself to be crippled by fear again. The other side of fear is exciting!

***

This phase of my awakening that I have been reminded of today upon waking up from a lovely sleep-in, I want to call the 'avatar phase'. When I would describe this feeling to the people around me, I would always reference the movie *Avatar* that Sam

Worthington stars in, as I felt the world within the movie represented how I am perceiving earth. If you haven't seen the movie *Avatar*, I highly recommend it. I would watch it on repeat when I was younger! To give you a brief rundown: It is a lush alien world called Pandora, where Na'vi people who appear primitive but are highly evolved live. The planet is poisonous to human so they create these human/Na'vi hybrids, called avatars. Jake Sully, a paralysed former Marine, becomes mobile again through an avatar and falls in lone with the planet's energy and soon realises all life within this planet is connected.

Visually, the movie is full of life, varying bright colours and is straight 'out of this world'. One day during the most intense stages of my spiritual awakening, I looked around at the trees blowing in the breeze, the sun beaming down with its power of light, and I felt like I had woken up on a completely different planet, like in *Avatar*. The energy and feelings that immersed my earthly body are near impossible to describe. I was overwhelmed with appreciation and in complete awe of the world around me. I felt immense excitement. Just like in *Avatar* when he discovers that all beings and life are connected through some divine universal flow of energy. It's amazing how much of a shift I had in perspective.

For the next few weeks, I spent a vast amount of time in nature, feeling and appreciating this intense sensation that I am finding difficult to express in words. I now noticed everything – the details of the clouds, the patterns on leaves, the sunbeams in the sky, rock shapes, the wind's force, and how incredible are clouds!? Seriously! I could go on all day, but I'm sure you're picking up what I'm putting down. However, not only did I notice all these little things, I felt them on a soul level. Writing this is making me feel these deep appreciative emotions. I am grateful for my awakening and the testing times that pushed me. For if I had not experienced the testing times, I would not be bathing in the awakened soul path. And I would not be sharing this with you. I wondered if this feeling would fade. Would I always have this immense appreciation for this planet we call home? I feel like I can say yes – this has become my natural state. However, it has lost the intensity that something new overwhelms us with. This feeling is something that I tune in to daily and is one of the major highlights on my awakening journey.

***

It's currently 11:51 on a Wednesday night. I tried to go to sleep at about 10 pm but I lay awake tossing and turning, unable to sleep, and this has become a common occurrence during my awakening. My bedtime seems to be getting later and later. Some weeks, prior to my awakening, I was a 9-to-9:30-pm-lights-out-as-soon-as-I-hit-the-pillow kind of person. I wanted to sleep as much as I could. I dreaded getting up in the morning and would even pull sickies to stay at home in bed. I would also be able to sleep-in all day if I wanted to. Now I lie awake most nights struggling to sleep. This is not because I'm stressed or anxious or anything along those lines. I cannot sleep because I'm so damn happy and excited about life!? Doesn't it sound wild! When my head hits the pillow, I am flooded with ideas and hopes for the future. I feel immense gratitude for where I am now, and occasionally reflect on the past and the events that led me to where I am today. I want to be up and out of bed early so I can embrace my day, and I can't sleep at night – just another confusing aspect of awakening, I guess. Overwhelming happiness and excitement rush through my body!

This is most definitely one of the many perks of awakening. Well ... the positive feelings aside, I wonder if this no-sleeping thing will stay? Am I going to be sleep-deprived forever? I still don't entirely understand this phase of awakening, and I'm not sure what its purpose is but I'm just flowing with it. It's one million times better than being up at night because I'm crying or hungry. Nothing worse than trying to sleep on an empty stomach. I felt this was just a nice and short little phase to add as I sat up yet again unable to sleep. Maybe in the future I will have some more answers as to why I get flooded this ... OMG, as I wrote that, I just got a little download from my spirit guides. One of the reasons I am not sleeping is because I'm not allowing enough time for stillness during the day so my guides are sending me all my guidance as I lie in stillness before sleep. I am not getting flooded with ideas and hopes for the future; I am receiving guidance! How did I not figure this out earlier?! I guess if I figured it out earlier, it wouldn't have ended up in my book, now, would it? Powerful stuff. How am I this lucky?!

***

It's crazy how once you step into your purpose, you become magnetic. I've noticed since I have stepped into my purpose, focused on living in alignment, and committed to raising my vibration and loving myself, that I've become strangely magnetic. I feel others have become drawn to my natural healing energy and good vibes. This may sound odd and I definitely don't want to sound up myself, but I feel my energy is highly contagious and super magnetic to those around me. I guess this is another bonus of awakening and committing to your growth. Men throw themselves at you – *hahaha*, just kidding, but not really. It's nuts. Surely one of these men is my soul mate, hey, universe? You wouldn't play me like that, now, would you?

Anyway, moving on. Everyone around me is responding to me in a hugely different way in comparison to before my awakening. I have random strangers cheering me on for my Raise Your Vibe program I have created online. People at the shops are friendlier – well, I don't have my resting bitch face on now but still counts. I have my friends and family telling me I'm 'glowing'. I have people at work complimenting me on my 'vibe' and 'energy'. It's incredible and I really feel this energy within me radiating out.

Since awakening, I feel like I'm glowing and it truly reflects onto my outside appearance. I feel more radiant and vibrant, and I am loving it! I am a completely different person to the person I was prior to my awakening, and everyone sees it. I hope this gets you excited for the times ahead of you on your own awakening journey, or maybe you are already at this incredible phase! Embrace it! Keep the good vibes flowing! When you embrace and love yourself from within, you radiate this and it's contagious!

***

Some days, I get super excited about new things I discover or new lessons I have learnt, or a test I've just passed that my higher self has given me, and I start to ramble on to my sister or dad. Sometimes the looks I get are of pure confusion. Some days, I don't even get looked at – *hahaha* – they just continue on about their business and give me some 'mmm, hmms'. I'll never forget the day I told my sister about one of my crazy past-life regression sessions where I saw myself in an old castle. I'm guessing it was in medieval times but I'm not 100% sure as I'm not a history buff, but I was wearing a tight, red corset dress, with my long, black hair running down my back, and I explained how I experienced my own peaceful death during that life. My sister flat out said to me this day, 'Sometimes I think you're on crack,' and that is *my reality of spirituality* right there. Some days, people think you're a beautiful glowing goddess living your damn best spiritual life. Other days, 'you're on crack'. *Haha*, fun times. The beauty of calling in your soul family is that even if they aren't around you, you can message them all your new discoveries and they completely understand, as they were most likely tripping out on one of their own past-life regression sessions twenty minutes prior.

By living at home whilst going through my awakening, I was gifted the chance to build stronger relationships with Dad and Ky. I spent most days avoiding them and hiding away prior to my awakening. As I became my truest self, everyone felt it. They felt my happiness, openness and love, and, in return, I got the same back. Dad and I have had deeper conversations than ever before, opening up about our experiences, things we have gone through and people within our lives. My relationship with Ky has also flourished. I no longer block her out. I no longer pick at her. She no longer torments me. We tell each other everything now and really bonded over the time when my break-up took over my life. It drew us closer than ever before, not to mention coronavirus forcing us to be each other's bestie whilst being trapped under the same roof as one another for weeks on end. We are soul sisters and share everything with each other now – no secrets and no judgements. The more I let Ky in, the more she lets me in, and the closer we become. I am more loving, more open and more connected to Dad and Ky than I have ever been. We are a much higher vibe, happier household now, closer than ever. My awakening made me realise how lucky I am to have Ky and Dad. I never felt this kind of gratitude prior to waking up. I hope that by living with Dad and Ky, and them being surrounded by my ever-growing consciousness, their own awakening is triggered, but we will see. Maybe this book will do it, or maybe they will just think I'm 'on crack' again.

***

Currently, I am raising my vibe daily! I am raising my vibe because it makes ME feel good! It's just a bonus that energy is contagious!

Little Life Update

I'm currently crying my eyes out at the dining table with my sister because she and her boyfriend of four and a half years just broke up. #EmpathLife

I'm in a huge state of processing and healing currently. The past week, I have dived into breath-work sessions and a kinesiology appointment, hoping for some movement out of the lower vibrational state I was in. Sunday night, after my committed week of healing, I arrived home from one of my many illegal beach trips, and Dad had been staying at his girlfriend's place for the past week, so I hadn't seen him. Dad took one look at me and told me that I 'looked really healthy' and was 'glowing'. In that moment, I could have cried. I felt so proud of myself and where I was at on my journey. I walked over to Dad and gave him a hug. Now, I know that this probably doesn't seem like a big deal, but past me would never have expressed the love I felt for Dad in that moment – I would have just held it in. I am sitting within this gratitude for my awakening and the gifts it has given me. I honestly don't know how I lived prior to waking up.

26

Not the End, the Beginning!

    You know how on movies and television shows you see writers experiencing writer's block? Amidst their struggles, they do anything they can to try to shake it – trying new exercise, eating new foods, anything to get the inspiration flowing and the words out onto their pages. This wasn't the case for me; my struggles were somewhat on the other end of the spectrum.

*   I have never experienced writer's block whilst writing this book! For me, it has been quite the opposite! I have been getting flooded with things channelling through me, at the worst times. Some days, it was overwhelming how much content would flow through me. For instance, right now, I am kneeling on my shower floor. Water is going everywhere while I hang one arm out the door into the cold air, struggling to write on the notepad Dad brought to me mid-shower. I made*

it sound like an emergency and that I needed a notepad asap before these thoughts left me. 'Dad, quick. The ideas are flowing. Bring me a pen and paper, please! Quick!' I yelled from the bathroom. I'm so grateful Dad is supportive enough of this book to get up off his comfy couch when I summon him for a pen and paper – so blessed.

One part of my shower notes, a source for much that has been written in this book. As soon as I decided to fully commit to this book, the universe repaid me with endless content. I'm getting bombarded with content; it's overwhelming. I'm writing one thing and another completely different thing is flowing through my head. See what I mean? Definitely no writer's block here!

Although I didn't struggle with a lack of words to write, I did struggle some days with all the emotional shadow work this book has brought to the surface, and my perfectionist self loved procrastinating due to the anxiety of my words not being good enough. So much has risen within me, some days, I was so exhausted, struggling to find the motivation to open my laptop, but I powered through it all. It's like the universe has been giving me all this energy to birth this book into the world. However, at times, I have been letting self-doubt and lack of motivation take over, causing this energy to turn into a feeling of anxiety, crippling me from moving forward. My strength was needed to push through this. This book has tested me. It has tested my commitment to growth, my self-discipline and healing. It has tested my trust within the universe. It has tested my trust within myself. It has broken me down, in the best way possible, and showed me my strength.

I have noticed most people don't commit to healing, growth

and connecting with their soul guidance. Most people don't want to improve their being and their lives, because you know what? It takes a whole lot of guts to level up and take full responsibility for the way your life is. Commonly, people choose to play a victim within this world, just like I did. They choose to believe that things are happening *to* them, instead of *for* them, but everything happens for our greater good. Honestly, the level of divine support I received in life once I decided to step into a soul-filled life is incredible.

Little quote from Ky today: 'You work on that book twelve hours a day and stay up all night.' Yep, it's a passion.

***

I feel after spilling all my shit onto these pages, I have hit a whole other level of healing that needed to be processed and released, unlike anything I have ever felt before. The weight on my chest is heavy. Over the past few weeks, I have been in a deep state of processing – you know, the good old processing of emotions before stepping into a whole new level of consciousness. I felt stuck. I couldn't quite shake this lower state. I was full of anxiety and it was killing my vibe. I wasn't sure why it was taking so long to get me to the next level. Then I realised that I needed to release everything I have written within this book, to be reborn. A closing of a chapter.

So late last night at 11 pm, in a bid to release and heal from all this energy I was feeling, I decided that taking an illegal trip down to the beach during our stage-four coronavirus lockdown was vital. During this time, we are not allowed to travel more than 5 km from our place of residence, and the beach is about 35 km from my home. We also had a curfew in place from 9 pm to 5 am. But that wasn't stopping my little criminal self. My pull to the ocean was far stronger and outweighed the possible $1500 fine I could have received. I needed to dip into the healing womb of the sea, to heal and release everything that's been processing within my being whilst writing this book. Plus, I wanted to harness the energy of the full moon to bring this book to a close. Before I left for this risky drive to the beach, I wrote down everything that I wanted to release and everything I wanted to bring into my life. I got everything off my chest, filling an A4 piece of paper on both sides.

After the nerve-racking but also exhilarating drive to the beach, I was ready to jump into the water. I just knew, in my soul, that the ocean would wash away this lower vibrational state and give me the clarity I needed. I hopped out of the car. The full moon was shining bright. It was a warm 22 degrees – the warmest night we have had in a long time. I sat down on the beach, right in front of the water. I closed my eyes and allowed the sand between my toes to ground me. I instantly knew this was where I needed to be. This was where I would step into my higher vibration. I stripped down to my bathers. I held my piece of paper within my hand as I started to walk into the water. I told myself as I went to dive into this icy-cold water that this was going to wash all my worries, concerns, and lower energies away, revealing my new life. I dove in, and whilst underwater, I let out the biggest scream whilst ripping my piece of paper to shreds, partly because it was freezing, but this was also my way of healing – fuck, it felt good. I dove under the water and screamed a couple more times. I felt like a new person as I turned and headed towards the shore. I felt as though I was reborn, stepping into the new me, as I placed both feet back on dry sand. I exhaled with a huge sigh, and I was bursting with a renewed love for life.

Jumping into the ocean, taking that leap, saying yes – I am now realising that this is where I need to end this book. *Hold up.* As I'm writing this, one of those little money spiders just appeared in front of my face, hanging from the ceiling from its web. If that's not a sign that this is the perfect time to end this book, then I don't know what is.

Writing this book has healed me in ways I cannot put into words. I have turned my wounds into wisdom that I will carry with me for lifetimes. Spiritual awakening is the best thing to ever happen to me! I allow myself to step into my soul daily. We are eternal spiritual beings having an earthly experience. How cool is that?

The past eight weeks of Melbourne's Covid-19 lockdown have been a blessing for me. Amid a worldwide pandemic, I have had the time and the space to write my book of impact. My crazy-lady notes have turned into a whole book, after all.

I am now twenty-four years old, still working part-time for a volume builder. I have now shut down KYLYN Design to continue chasing the spiritual life every spare moment I can. I am still single and loving it; getting to know myself is so empowering. I still love sitting on the shower floor for all my greatest ideas. I still love long drives alone. I definitely still think I'm hilarious. I am planning to chase the sun, sand and sea in the coming months. Melbourne's lockdown is coming to an end. I have loved this time of realisation, transformation and healing.

This book has released me from the façade I once presented to the world. My vulnerability is my gift to you.

My journey has been brutal, to say the least. It wasn't all sunshine, yoga, a beautiful meditation, with a side of gratitude all whilst sipping on a matcha green tea to start each happy day. My reality was growing up with an alcoholic, rolling a car, having a miscarriage, falling ill with blood clots in my lungs, and experiencing my first heartbreak. It sure wasn't pretty. I had some really bad times. I was that chronic over-thinker, drowning in fear, guilt, anger and shame. Some days, I could not see any light. I was a lost girl, trapped so deep in her ego, full of self-doubt, confined to a box of limiting beliefs, and living a life extremely out of alignment. I was unconscious, unfulfilled, unhappy, depressed, anxious, lost and seeking answers. It was a choice to rise from my challenges. I gained some insight and awareness, creating shifts and breakthroughs, and realised I was waking up. Then doubt hit me, forcing me to face my shadow self and heal, pushing past beliefs and conditioning, to invite in the light. And now I am living an awakened present life, full of love, happiness and excitement to live. My reality gifted me my spiritual awakening, changing my life. I hold no anger or malice for the people or situations that shaped me. I send love to all who have been a part of these experiences in my life because they have blessed me into who I am, and I love me and I fucking love life! I have shifted my mindset, raised my vibe and changed my life forever! I am closing this chapter of my life.

I don't believe awakening needs to occur through trauma, pain and grief. You can learn and change in an undesirable state like I did, or you can grow and change in a state of optimism, excitement and joy, like I do the majority of the time now. Spiritual awakening does not always have to be triggered by hardship. Awakening can occur through pure awareness. My awakening shifted me into a place where I allow myself the space to grow and flourish. I am not afraid to sit within my emotions – this is expansion. I am embracing where I am at on my journey. I am happier than I have ever been. I have found my laugh. I no longer identify with my ego. I am an awakened soul, continually awakening and living a soul-filled life, trying my best to be flowing in alignment, and my relationships are better than ever. My mind has never been as quiet as it is at this stage of my life, and overthinking no longer cripples me. This freedom from the mind is one of the greatest gifts I have given myself. Of course, I have off days, but I power through, trusting the universe! I feel what I need to feel, and I release it! My vibrational set point is much higher, and it continues to rise as I heal. I pride myself on the energy and vibe I put out into this world. I have found my purpose. I am a healer, and I am filled with gratitude and overwhelmed with excitement to see where this path takes me. This book is my power of transformation. This book has healed me in many ways. This book was the creative outlet my soul longed for.

You don't need to see spirituality in a certain way, or feel you need to do certain things to be 'spiritual' and you don't even need to be 'spiritual' to shift into your best damn life! You can live your best life and not meditate. You can be spiritual and love coffee. You can say 'fuck'. You can love materialistic things, and you don't need to talk to spirit guides or tap into psychic abilities. And I swear, you can wear deodorant, or don't – entirely up to you. Remember, we are all just doing the best we can. Don't be hard on yourself or others. Spirituality is whatever you want it to be. Follow YOUR truth. Do what feels good for YOU! Connect to your inner knowing and trust! Because you always know the way.

My reality of spirituality is leaving my home at 11 pm, and driving 35 km to the beach to dip my body into the soothing ocean during a full moon and a coronavirus lockdown. It's yelling at my spirit guides when I'm driving because I have no idea what all the numbers I'm being repetitively shown mean. It's pulling two sick days from my part-time job because it's a full moon and I want to bathe in its power to finish my book. It's crouching on the floor crying amongst all my belongings that no longer feel like mine as I toss away over 60% of everything I own. It's placing my little house of security up for sale as I choose to embody freedom and adventure. It's releasing and closing the chapter on my old life as my book comes to an end. It's being so happy and excited about life, I can't sleep for a week.

The truth long held within me for lifetimes has now been expressed. I have made many shifts within myself through the writing of this book. The voice of the soul is like no other. Through creative expression, my throat chakra was cracked open. This book is me releasing, healing and stepping into my new life. By tapping into my power within and the messages my soul held, I have healed myself and the people whom this book touches.

Everything radiates from within you. You have the power to feel happiness and love, no matter what your external reality looks like. You are light. You are love. You are whole. You can do whatever the hell you want to do in this world! Embrace where you are at! Stand in your power! Expand! Believe in yourself! Believe in the universe! The world is pure magic! Leap! Wake up and choose to live your best damn life! You are magic! You are unique! You are powerful! Always remember, the universe has your back! There is a whole new life beyond fear, beliefs and ego. I am sending you so much love and light – breathe it in.

Activate your inner power! Recite: *I am powerful. I am whole. I am beautiful. I am unique. I am happy. I am connected. I am extraordinary. I am open to receiving from the universe. I am magnetic. I am soul. I am light. I am love.*

xxx

The reality of spirituality is yours to create

If this book has helped you along your journey, please share it with a friend or loved one. You never know the impact it may have on their life.

www.ingramcontent.com/pod-product-compliance
Lightning Source LLC
Chambersburg PA
CBHW021949290426
44108CB00012B/1001